D0772521

Actionable Intelligence

A Guide to Delivering Business Results with Big Data Fast!

Keith B. Carter

with contributions

from **Donald Farmer**
and **Clifford Siegel**

WILEY

Cover image: Wiley
Cover design: Wiley

Copyright © 2014 by John Wiley & Sons, Inc. All rights reserved.

Published by John Wiley & Sons, Inc., Hoboken, New Jersey.
Published simultaneously in Canada.

No part of this publication may be reproduced, stored in a retrieval system, or transmitted in any form or by any means, electronic, mechanical, photocopying, recording, scanning, or otherwise, except as permitted under Section 107 or 108 of the 1976 United States Copyright Act, without either the prior written permission of the Publisher, or authorization through payment of the appropriate per-copy fee to the Copyright Clearance Center, Inc., 222 Rosewood Drive, Danvers, MA 01923, (978) 750-8400, fax (978) 646-8600, or on the Web at www.copyright.com. Requests to the Publisher for permission should be addressed to the Permissions Department, John Wiley & Sons, Inc., 111 River Street, Hoboken, NJ 07030, (201) 748-6011, fax (201) 748-6008, or online at http://www.wiley.com/go/permissions.

Limit of Liability/Disclaimer of Warranty: While the publisher and author have used their best efforts in preparing this book, they make no representations or warranties with respect to the accuracy or completeness of the contents of this book and specifically disclaim any implied warranties of merchantability or fitness for a particular purpose. No warranty may be created or extended by sales representatives or written sales materials. The advice and strategies contained herein may not be suitable for your situation. You should consult with a professional where appropriate. Neither the publisher nor author shall be liable for any loss of profit or any other commercial damages, including but not limited to special, incidental, consequential, or other damages.

For general information on our other products and services or for technical support, please contact our Customer Care Department within the United States at (800) 762-2974, outside the United States at (317) 572-3993 or fax (317) 572-4002.

Wiley publishes in a variety of print and electronic formats and by print-on-demand. Some material included with standard print versions of this book may not be included in e-books or in print-on-demand. If this book refers to media such as a CD or DVD that is not included in the version you purchased, you may download this material at http://booksupport.wiley.com. For more information about Wiley products, visit www.wiley.com.

Library of Congress Cataloging-in-Publication Data:
Carter, Keith B., 1973-
   Actionable intelligence : a guide to delivering business results with big data fast! / Keith B. Carter with contributions from Donald Farmer and Clifford Siegel.
      1 online resource.
   Includes bibliographical references and index.
   Description based on print version record and CIP data provided by publisher; resource not viewed.
   ISBN 978-1-118-92060-2 (ebk); ISBN 978-1-118-92065-7 (ebk);
ISBN 978-1-118-91523-3   1. Decision making.   2. Strategic planning.   3. Big data.
   I. Title.
   HD30.23
   658.4'038028557—dc23

                                                                                    2014027154

Printed in the United States of America

10 9 8 7 6 5 4 3 2 1

Further Praise for *Actionable Intelligence*

"BI starts with an attempt to ask the right business questions until the answers reach an actionable outcome. This book reminds us to begin with back to basics before we jump into developing what users ask for. Keith calls it 'The Initial Answers.' From my experience, within-memory technology and advance visualization, businesses may no longer have to 'peel the onion' or drill down to reach the Actionable BI. Bringing together the power of BI and the business knowledge of the users is the ideation process Keith describes in his book."

—Elizabeth Lim, Vice President & CIO, Enterprise Information Management, STATS ChipPAC Ltd

"Big data is the buzzword these days; there is not a week passing through without an article, a blog, a discussion around this topic. There is no denying the fact that data, and if big even better, offer a big potential for business people. But is this enough? Surely not. . . . Through the book, Keith, Cliff, and Donald will guide you through this data jungle and enable you to unveil the full potential of your data for actionable intelligence. Do yourself a favour, read it!"

—Roxane Desmicht, Senior Director, Corporate Supply Chain, Infineon Technologies

"Only a few years ago, the ability to have access to data across a global enterprise was the challenge. Leaders struggled to make decisions in the absence of near time information. Fast forward to the present, and those same leaders are still challenged to make decisions—because there is too much data. Actionable Intelligence provides a road map to navigating the big-data space to provide decisions and, more importantly, results. Kudos to Keith Carter and team in sharing their career passion and lessons learned."

—Edward DuBeau, Sr. Director, ERP, Zoetis

"This book, Actionable Intelligence, is a fantastic resource in shifting our energy from delivery of technology to delivery of insight and organizational outcomes. Whether new to BI or a seasoned veteran, Actionable

Intelligence provides a 'how to,' or reflective assessment, on how we as BI professionals add real value."

—Stuart Ward, Platform Manager: Business Intelligence
and Reporting, ANZ Bank

"Actionable intelligence represents the next frontier of innovation. Decision makers would be wise to empower their operations to harness effectively actionable intelligence to gain a competitive advantage. Actionable intelligence promises to level the playing field among profit-seeking enterprises, regardless of size. This book offers a glimpse into paradigm-shifting approaches that every business owner ignores at its peril."

—Justin Swindells, Patent Attorney

"So much of the hype about Big Data has led organizations to expend large sums of money with relatively little return on their investment or to wallow in the slough of despair as they try to figure out all they want to know. This book from a highly experienced and skilled practitioner working within a global context cuts through all the nonsense with delineated action steps, sage advice, and insights from many different practical situations. Carter's key point is that Big Data is ONLY useful when it provides actionable intelligence that informs decisions and guides responses. It grows by accretion as more and more insights are derived and delivered with impact across the organization. This book will be sheet music for the practiced eyes and ears of senior management and an open entrée for data practitioners within enterprises to become more central to core operations that increase competitiveness in complex global markets with their ever changing parameters and issues. Larger nonprofit and government agency leaders can also glean many useful insights from this volume. This is a must-read for 2014 and beyond for senior leaders, managers across the enterprise, and those leading work in applied data fields."

—Dennis Cheek, Ph.D., Executive Director, National Creativity
Network, USA, Co-Chair, Global Creativity United,
and Visiting Professor, Innovation and Entrepreneurship,
IESEG School of Management, France

Dedicated to my late mom, Mary Kennedy Carter,
and my dad, Donald Wesley Carter Sr.
Their life and love is a source of constant inspiration.
This book is also dedicated
to you and people like you
who want to help others make better decisions.

Contents

Preface

What's actionable intelligence?

In speaking around the world on the topic of making better decisions using facts, I've found again and again that leaders from all industries yearn for more information. They want to be able to assess risks and opportunities quickly and efficiently. They want answers in enough time to be able to make a difference. They want to seize opportunities. They need intelligence that is on time and accurate. They want what I call "actionable intelligence."

A Vision of What Could Be: The Hospital Information System

As I was beginning my own journey into actionable intelligence, my mother had a stroke. Her stroke led me to understand the real need for intelligence in a transformative way.

It was a gray day in early 2010. I was on my way to my office at the Estée Lauder Companies, Inc. in Melville, New York, where I was working in a global role establishing an intelligence organization, running the project management office (PMO) for supply chain, managing Sarbanes-Oxley and customs compliance, and implementing operational efficiencies throughout the business.

As I drove to the office, my head was filled with thoughts of supply chain intelligence. My thoughts were interrupted when my cell phone started ringing.

It was my father.

"Son, I'm at the hospital. Your mother fainted in the bathroom this morning and I couldn't revive her."

Silence. . . .

I asked, "Where are you? What hospital?"

"Please come to South Nassau Community Hospital," he responded.

When I arrived at the hospital, my mother, Mary, was sitting up in bed, looking a bit weak.

The doctor told me, "Your mother had a stroke."

She looked fine, but could only mouth words to us. She could not speak. Miraculously, she began to speak about 30 minutes later and was able to move her arm. We spent the rest of the day at the hospital, waiting and wondering.

At about 6:30 the next morning, as I was making my way out of my house, my cell phone rang. It was a nurse at the hospital.

"Mr. Carter, come quickly to the hospital," he said. "Your mother had another stroke."

I was numb.

I immediately called my dad and drove over to the hospital.

When I arrived at my mom's bedside, she couldn't speak, she couldn't move the right side of her body or her left arm. As she was poked and prodded by the doctors, she didn't visibly react to any pain.

Tears came to my eyes. Here was my mom—my hero for life—now with a contorted face and unable to speak or move.

I became greatly concerned. What efforts would be made to support my mother?

I asked for information—basic things, such as what we could expect medications to do to help my mother. The hospital staff responded coldly: "We are busy. Later we will try to give you the information."

I pushed for more: "How did this second stroke happen? What do the MRI and X-rays look like?"

They responded, "We don't have that information. Go to records downstairs."

I did, but to see the records I had to stand in line and pay. I received the images on a disk in a format I couldn't immediately view.

In fact, I ran into roadblocks that prevented me from gathering facts at every turn.

It was difficult to find doctors who would explain the situation, and nurses were at best impatient and often downright mean. (I would realize later that their frustration stemmed from being worked hard and lacking information themselves to respond to customers like me.)

The situation was beyond frustrating. I just couldn't access information fast enough, and relatives from all over the country were asking me again and again, "What's the status?" "How's Mary?" "What medicines is she taking?" "How often?" "When?" "How much?" "With what?" "What are the side-effects?"

And so on and so on.

I became information central. I set up conference calls at specific times for my relatives to provide information so I wouldn't have to call 50 people individually. However, these calls were very frustrating because I was stuck between a hospital that didn't readily share updates about my mother and family members who wanted to be totally involved in her care. They were all concerned, and so was I. We wanted facts so we could understand and improve the situation.

Thankfully, an angel and dear family friend, Dr. Linda Huang, helped us move my mom to Columbia University Presbyterian Hospital (Columbia for short).

Each case of moving a patient from one hospital to another is different, but typically, the accepting physician reviews the case and assesses the risk versus the benefits of moving the patient. Thankfully, Linda, a graduate of Columbia Dentistry and assistant professor of the same, was able to make it happen.

Columbia was amazing! I drove there following the ambulance. When I arrived and saw my mother being taken care of, I immediately approached a doctor. He took the time to walk my father and me through her case.

I had been trying to understand the medications prescribed to my mother at the other hospital, but the nurses and doctors were always too busy there. When I asked the doctors at Columbia, they said, "Wait one moment." And, indeed, in just minutes, they presented a chart of medications. The chart explained the indications, contraindications, side effects, timing, and dosages of all the medications. Wow! Talk about instant information.

It was amazing; the hospital staff had time to spend with me and had all the information they needed at their fingertips.

Later, I would ask the doctors more questions—specifically, about the MRI that I never saw at the previous hospital. You will recall that the previous hospital gave us a CD that could be viewed only using specific hospital software—and cost me time and money to receive.

The Columbia doctor took me over to a workstation in the hallway. These workstations were located throughout the hospital. He logged in, entered my mother's information, and immediately brought up all her records. He showed me the MRI on the spot, and calmly and respectfully showed me the infarction (dead part of the brain) and explained its impact.

I didn't have to go to a separate records department. I didn't have to wait in line. I didn't have to pay. And, importantly, I could immediately view and understand the information. Why? Because the information was at the doctor's fingertips. And, he took time to explain everything to me in a way that had meaning.

The hospital information system was so powerful at Columbia that anytime I wanted information I could simply ask and it was given. Staff could just as easily access information.

I was very impressed, and my family was pleased with the understanding that this new flow of information enabled. The level of care at Columbia was remarkably more engaging and patient-oriented—all because of information.

It was this hospital experience that propelled me toward a journey to actionable intelligence capabilities: instant access to forward-looking information on everyone's desktops.

Benefits of Actionable Intelligence

As a business leader or a business function lead, you have customers. Don't you want to be able to find information about a specific request from a customer immediately? Just as Columbia University Presbyterian

Hospital has thousands of patients, you might have thousands of orders. The ability to find the right information for a customer at the right moment—and to be able to immediately explain the information—earns you so much trust and faith, it is impossible to measure the benefit.

Without the kind of hospital information system that Columbia University Presbyterian has, when someone asks a question you likely have to say, "Let me call you back," then research the information, which possibly involves e-mailing other people. (Hopefully, they will send a response.) This is an issue because people are impatient and very busy. The reason they are asking your business a question is because they want to know the information right now, not 30 minutes later and certainly not days later.

Think about the soft benefits of having answers at your fingertips:

- You don't have to take as much time to answer the customer.
- The customer has more confidence in your ability to deliver.
- Expectations can be set quickly.

The hard benefits:

- When you share the information, you can react to the customer's request and achieve hard benefits right away by adjusting the order if they need more or less.
- More broadly, all plans can be adjusted to take into account all the known information at all times, leading to real savings and increased efficiency at a relatively small cost.

For a concrete example of what actionable intelligence can do, consider this quote from a product director in a large fast-moving consumer goods company.

> We've been carefully tracking an important product launch, worth $55.6 million in the next 12 months. The actionable intelligence tool showed me the global forecast has increased by 160,000 pieces globally for the next six months in the last four weeks alone, a $10 million increase. This information enables us to stay ahead of the demand increases and proactively coordinate a response, reducing costs and ensuring we don't go out of stock and avoiding airfreight.

See the difference? Speed and results! Readily available information for decisions enables proactive actions and creates heroes like this product director.

Actionable intelligence capabilities can result in massive benefits for you, your coworkers, your boss, your customers—basically, everybody related to the company. Let this book be the guide on your journey, and you may soon find yourself the next actionable intelligence hero.

Now please join me for a good walk on the journey to delivering actionable intelligence.

How to Use This Book

The book is written as a guide for sharing best practices, emphasizing key points, and defending effective intelligence methodologies. Business managers can use it to work with IT and say, "Look here! We can work together like this." I also expect IT to be able to use it to run to senior management and say, "Hey! We can be really good partners with you on delivering sales."

When stuck on how to visualize data or tell a story, pull out this book and follow the ideation methodology.

At the end of each chapter is a section called "Summary and Considerations."

There you will find:

- A Point to Ponder
- A Quote to Remember
- A Question to Consider

To evolve the concept of actionable intelligence, I encourage you to share your thoughts, ideas, and experiences. You can do so on my website: www.keithbcarter.com.

Acknowledgments

Big hugs and thanks to my wonderful wife, Stella, and our boys, Emmanuel and Luke, who were all very supportive as I wrote this book. My boys listened to it as a bedtime story.

With great thanks to my friends, mentors, and family, who have changed my life in small and big ways.

A special thanks to Jessica Foong, Wen Wei Zhao, and Mike Van Den Eijden for their special work.

I thank God for granting me the experiences in actionable intelligence so I can share them with you in this book.

A special thanks goes to Debra Donston-Miller, who helped sand off the rough edges from this book.

I would also like to mention the following people who contributed to the book in their own special way:

Yuri Aguiar

Ed Dubeau

Dennis Cheek

Haley Garner

Rayna Fagen

Naveed Husain
Jason Schogel
Ser Aik
Jason Mayberg
Naveed Husain
Mike Saliter
Hideki Sakai
Rocky Russell
Helena May

Teresa Kennedy
The SCI team
And IT people around the world!

Introduction

My hope is that readers come away from this book with the realization that they can improve the lives of others by giving them the answers they need to make better decisions faster and easier.

When team members have usable information at their fingertips, they can:

- Answer questions faster, with little or no effort needed to collect the data.
- Make better use of their time, planning improved outcomes.
- Make improvements for the future, instead of dwelling on past failures.

If actionable intelligence sounds a lot like business intelligence, it's no wonder.

Using this book as a guide, you can play a part in making a positive impact on your colleagues by achieving the dream that business intelligence (BI) has promised since the term was first coined way back in 1858.

BI tools are the same across industries, whether you are helping a business, government, or nonprofit. BI concepts can also be helpful for individuals who want to make revolutionary change.

1

While they are very different in the end, both BI and actionable intelligence start with a question.

When a new question is raised, time is of the essence; the intelligence organization needs to respond quickly. However, due to the rigidness of the system and lack of focus in the organization or the governance methodology, it can be difficult to make the changes necessary to arrive at a complete decision.

For example, analysis might be performed in Excel, because a business user requires additional factors or information. The results will likely be presented in PowerPoint—with static data points that are as limited in usability as when the project began.

For years, the smartest minds in BI have struggled with how to deliver forward-looking answers to improve outcomes. Vendors and consultants have recommended how to leverage "regular" data—and now big data.

The promise is a single source of truth. *If* we can get all the data into one place, with no data duplication, only *then* will we be able to visualize the data and reach information nirvana.

Actually, a single source of truth may actually introduce risk. The answers look so perfect and precise that they tempt people into making decisions that should really require more thought and additional data enrichment from various sources.

For the past 15 years, dedicated, hard-working teams have churned out BI reports but missed the mark on the original vision of business intelligence.

I offer an alternative approach to achieving incredible results from business intelligence:

- Live and work with purpose to improve the lives of others by giving them the answers they need to make better decisions faster and more easily.
- Deliver sustainable improvements in agility, impact, cost savings, improved quality, excellent customer service, and more.
- Build a team of passionate and purpose-driven organization members to identify the burning platform(s) and share a vision of "what good looks like."
- Work with these "doers" and start delivering iterative answers. Cut out the "talkers."

- Build the benefits case with quick wins.
- Watch out for cultural and political challenges that get in the way of sharing data, sharing intelligence, and sharing success and recognition.
- Allow for mistakes.
- Be open to changing course, vision, and focus, if needed.
- Do whatever it takes to deliver results.

I also challenge you to think about whether your organization has capabilities to:

- View forward-looking metrics answering: What will our business performance look like in the future according to our plans?
- Answer a customer's questions about their orders without e-mailing others for information.
- Instantly understand the impact of a catastrophe on the business.
- Regularly validate the data quality (timeliness and accuracy) on a visible dashboard.
- Run strategy meetings with the data needed to make fact-based decisions without stressing out your organization by requiring them to cobble data together into Excel.

If your company can do all of these things, it is far ahead of most, according to a *Harvard Business Review* study of Fortune 1000 companies and large government agencies ("Who's Really Using Big Data" by Paul Barth and Randy Bean, September 12, 2012).

The study stated that:

- Only 15 percent of respondents ranked their access to data today as adequate or world-class.
- Only 21 percent of respondents ranked their intelligence capabilities as adequate or world-class.
- Only 17 percent of respondents ranked their ability to use data and intelligence to transform their business as more than adequate or world-class.

I have seen the same thing in my own studies here in Singapore. During the Big Data World Conference September 2013, Dr. Jussi Keppo and I ran a big data clinic in which we encouraged conference participants to write down their key learnings, strategic business questions, and capability gaps.

More than 60 percent felt they did not have the people capability to gain benefits from big data—in either business or IT.

More than 40 percent felt data accuracy and data sharing were problems that prevented them from getting the answers they needed to make better decisions.

This book will enable you to leverage the power of big data by developing an actionable intelligence ecosystem to manage data, visualize it and use it to:

- Answer strategic business questions at the speed needed to make a difference.
- Identify execution issues and improve agility.
- Provide forward visibility in enough time to improve business outcomes.

You will learn how several multinational corporations delivered real business benefits and many soft benefits using actionable intelligence.

By the end of the book you will be able to envision, budget, implement, and deliver similar benefits at your own organization.

Enjoy the journey!

Chapter 1

Vision of Actionable Intelligence

Key Points and Questions

- For intelligence to have value it must deliver answers in time to make a difference to business outcomes.
- The availability of big data is not an immediate way to improve your business.
- Before jumping to statistical packages and hiring data scientists, make sure business leaders have visibility into the intelligence you already have in hand.
- Statistical models that are missing large sets of data and don't include influencing data never predict the future; they can be used only to neatly outline past mistakes.

According to Chinese folklore, around 170 A.D., China's Han Dynasty was very weak. As a result, lawlessness and corruption were rampant throughout the land. One man, Liu Bei, and his friends swore to bring peace to the land by unifying the country and reestablishing the emperor. This task proved to be difficult, so they turned to an adviser renowned for his wisdom, Zhuge Liang. Together, they set out on an expedition to create an alliance with a general named Zhou Yu, who controlled one-third of China. But Zhou Yu, knowing that Zhuge Liang was critical to the success of his enemies, sought to trick him into taking on an impossible task as a way to prove loyalty to the proposed alliance. The true purpose was to trick Zhuge Liang into unwillingly signing up for his own death.

The task was to create 100,000 arrows in 10 days or face execution by General Zhou Yu. One hundred thousand arrows in 10 days sounds like an absolutely impossible task for any ordinary man. Zhuge Liang would surely face death, right?

But he was a resourceful and wise hero. Here's what he did: He prepared 20 boats with straw puppets and straw bales on the sides, and a few men inside. He knew the night he sailed his ships into battle would be particularly foggy. Zhuge Liang made his men sail just close enough to be heard but remain unseen. Then he had his men light some torches, beat the drums, and shout orders to the few men actually on board the 20 ships to sound like a large force coming for attack.

Zhuge Liang foresaw the warlord Cao Cao's response: Cao Cao quickly ordered his archers to move out and start shooting toward the drum sounds and torches. Volley upon volley, he and his men fired away. The arrows from the archers got stuck in the straw figures on the boat and the straw bales on the sides. When Zhuge Liang's boats were loaded on one side with arrows and threatened to tilt under the weight, he ordered the ships turned 180 degrees to catch arrows with the straw bales on the other side of the boat.

With more than enough arrows and dawn beginning to break, he ordered the ships to sail back to Zhou Yu.

So what did Zhuge Liang end up with? One hundred thousand arrows and his life, and all the while he sat drinking wine in his cabin on the ship. And Cao Cao? He hadn't really been attacked, but he was outsmarted nonetheless.

Zhou Yu's plan to kill Zhuge Liang through trickery had failed, and this later resulted in his own downfall.

The difference among the three men was their use of information—intelligence, to be more precise.

Zhuge Liang knew what was going on. He knew it was going to be foggy. He knew what his task was, and knew what Cao Cao's reaction would be when he was confronted with Zhuge Liang's trap. He combined this knowledge and performed extraordinarily, against all odds.

Zhuge Liang had a 360-degree view of both the internal and external environment. And he acted accordingly. By contrast, Cao Cao was literally left in the dark throughout the supposed attack, and Zhou Yu had taken a gamble on Zhuge Liang's knowledge without knowing the facts about Zhuge Liang's capabilities.

Most businesses nowadays are in the position of Cao Cao: They lack visibility into what is truly happening in the business environment and make quick, snap reactions to what is happening around them. They are not at all proactive; they are not leveraging the environment. Instead, they are manipulated by the environment.

The Challenge at Hand

Today, more than ever, information is everywhere around us. Indeed, we are bombarded with information. We all know, for example, that Facebook, Twitter, and LinkedIn are sources of information about our social lives. Though the different apps and sites in this field all offer different forms of social media, they have one thing in common: They let people create information and allow them to read everyone else's information.

For example, by participating on Facebook, you always know what is happening in your social circle via posts on your Facebook wall and updates from others. Some information is useful; some is useless. However, in the end, you always know what is going on because everything is conveniently posted in a single spot: the Facebook wall.

Businesses operate by receiving a tremendous amount of information but usually lack the central, company-wide "Facebook wall" to see it all at any one time.

The process of gathering information from others is often long and painstaking instead of instant and easy. Where businesses would benefit significantly from having all the information they need at their fingertips to provide answers, most are still struggling to pull together the most basic data. Some even lack common definitions and use data sets requiring cumbersome translations to see a global result.

However, if employees know all the latest social updates, why can the same employees not know all the latest information about their own companies?

There is a similar disconnect with mobile.

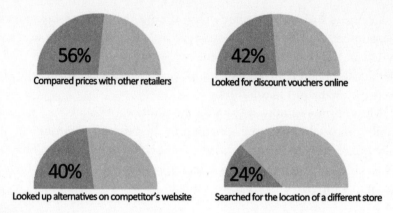

Figure 1.1   How Consumers Shop

What data do you need to respond quickly to your customers or leaders? How quickly can you access it? Is it accessible on a secure mobile device?

When customers walk into retail stores they have a wealth of knowledge about the products they are considering purchasing. In Figure 1.1, 63 percent of smartphone owners are checking the prices of the products while they browse, a process called "showrooming." The data they get from their mobile devices helps them to decide where and when to buy products.

Think about this process and how people shopped just a couple of years ago. It is a huge change. Why should corporate employees not expect the same level of change in their own organizations?

If consumers can go through a significant process change to adapt to the latest big data technology to use actionable intelligence without any formal training, why can these consumers not do the same when they arrive at work?

For today's businesses that is the challenge: change. Think about the difference honestly. Is it:

- Complacency to accept the current situation, even though that situation could be improved massively?
- That your company is using systems that just are not as fast and easy as using Facebook?
- That your company has implemented processes and incentives that are inadequate for driving a change in behavior?

Let us start by illustrating just how painful and dire the current situation is for modern-day companies, especially those that are larger in size.

Typically, supply chain senior management needs to go several levels down the chain and interact with a team of people just to figure out if and when a market will receive its shipments. This is due to how widely dispersed the information is.

Figure 1.2 is a sample e-mail chain—one that you might find in any supply chain organization. (Any resemblance to actual emails is purely coincidental.)

Some of the details of Figure 1.2 follow.

——Original Message——
From: Singapore Sales
Sent: October 15, 2009
To: APAC Regional Forecaster
Cc:
Subject: Takashimiya Wants Additional 30% for Valentine's Day
Exciting news! Our customer wants 30% more than the original order. Can we have it?

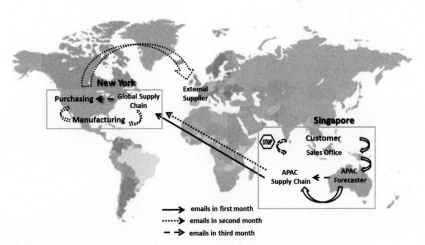

Figure 1.2   E-mails around the World in 90 Days

——Original Message——
From: APAC Sales
Sent: October 15, 2009
To: APAC Regional Forecaster, APAC Supply Chain
Cc:
Subject: Takashimiya Wants Additional 30% for Valentine's Day
Can you help get more products for this customer?

——Original Message——
From: APAC Supply Chain
Sent: October 18, 2009
To: NY Supply Chain
Cc: APAC Forecaster
Subject: Takashimiya Wants Additional 30% for Valentine's Day
Let me check with NY Supply chain. NY can you provide an answer to this request?

——Original Message——
From: NY Supply Chain
Sent: November 3, 2009
To: APAC Supply Chain
Cc:
Subject: Takashimiya Wants Additional 30% for Valentine's Day
Let me check who makes it and follow up with them.

——Original Message——
From: APAC Supply Chain
Sent: November 10, 2009
To: NY Supply Chain
Cc:
Subject: Takashimiya Wants Additional 30% for Valentine's Day
Please respond? The customer really wants to know.

——Original Message——
From: NY Supply Chain
Sent: November 28, 2009
To: APAC Supply Chain
Cc:
Subject: Takashimiya Wants Additional 30% for Valentine's Day
I found out the product is made in Long Island. [This would have required checking at least four systems or contacting four people in each major manufacturing location.]

——Original Message——
From: NY Supply Chain
Sent: November 28, 2009
To: NY Manufacturing
Cc:
Subject: Takashimiya Wants Additional 30% for Valentine's Day
Can you support making a quantity of this much for this item code?

——Original Message——
From: NY Manufacturing
Sent: December 2, 2009
To: NY Supply Chain
Cc:
Subject: Takashimiya Wants Additional 30% for Valentine's Day
We don't have enough components. Let me check with the supplier, but I have to go through the purchasing group.

——Original Message——
From: NY Manufacturing
Sent: December 3, 2009
To: NY Purchasing
Cc: NY Supply Chain
Subject: Takashimiya Wants Additional 30% for Valentine's Day
Can the supplier provide additional XYZ components?

——Original Message——
From: NY Supply Chain
Sent: December 15, 2009
To: NY Purchasing,
Cc: NY Manufacturing
Subject: Takashimiya Wants Additional 30% for Valentine's Day
Purchasing, please respond

——Original Message——
From: APAC Supply Chain
Sent: January 3, 2010
To: NY Supply Chain
Cc:
Subject: Takashimiya Wants Additional 30% for Valentine's Day
Do you have a response yet?

——Original Message——
From: NY Supply Chain
Sent: January 5, 2010
To: APAC Supply Chain
Cc:
Subject: Takashimiya Wants Additional 30% for Valentine's Day
No, still waiting for Long Island Manufacturing who is waiting for purchasing, who is waiting for the supplier.

——Original Message——
From: APAC Supply Chain
Sent: February 10, 2010 5:15 PM
To: NY Supply Chain
Cc: APAC Forecasting, Singapore Sales
Subject: Takashimiya Wants Additional 30% for Valentine's Day
Please cancel this request. The retailer had to fill the spot with other products.

Painful to read, isn't it?

All of these e-mails might suggest a highly complicated issue, but the problem is quite simple: lack of answers.

It was really difficult to determine:

- Who made the product
- The product's status
- Which suppliers provided components
- Who was responsible for delivering results

Worst of all, there was no performance benchmark that would incent all involved to provide better service in the future.

All over the world, customers and sales teams desperately ask when they will receive their shipments. All the while, the supply chain struggles to provide the needed answers. Sales and operations battle over the right numbers for forecasts, inventory, and customer service.

These meetings can sometimes become emotional and demoralizing.

Luckily, some companies have recognized the situation and agreed they need to do something about it. These companies realize that they need information that can be trusted. Information that is aggregated, ready to access, and easy to comprehend. Information they can act on—in other words, actionable intelligence.

The Big Data Lie

Business leaders and employees hear that moving from an organization that is completely opaque to one in which information is readily available undergo a world of change. Decision making will no longer be based on guesswork, hunches, or random facts. Instead, it will be based on good, clean, valuable pieces of information that are ready for action. That is what companies nowadays are striving for.

Armed with this knowledge, companies jump in and start collecting big data—extremely large and comprehensive data sets—to investigate and draw conclusions from. However, this is the wrong first step because raw data says nothing by itself, and placing even more data into bigger databases or copying data into spreadsheets provides no value. This is simply more of the same. Leaders and employees still won't have answers; instead, they will have data—more data than they had before, but not the kind of data or the approach to data that would make their lives easier.

Another mistake is to start by cleaning up the data and categorizing every bit of it. There is value to cleaning up data. Indeed, there is benefit to normalizing data by centralizing, classifying, and structuring it. However, it's hard to make a business case to do this because when the cleaning and organizing is done, the data does not provide answers to business questions. This is especially true when it turns into an IT-focused project that doesn't gain the assurance from users that the data has been validated and is usable.

The right approach is to start with a strategic business question and acquire the data to answer that question. Only then can you quickly start visualizing your business, performing business discovery, and delivering actionable intelligence. You will provide information that people can act on because it is complete, true, and readily available. The actionable intelligence approach works iteratively, starts small, and grows. All the while, it delivers answers to the strategic business questions.

Actionable Intelligence: The Road and the Destination

Today, the benefits from the massive quantities of data we generate are only realized when that data is processed using a growing array of visualization tools. Simple spreadsheets and software such as QlikView, SAP Visual Intelligence, and SAS provide a dynamic visualization of big data, uncovering the myriad links and interconnections behind the information.

It is also helpful when data is stored in well-understood systems like Microsoft SQL Server. However, with big data, performance can become an issue that necessitates making a move to Hadoop, Google Big Query, or SAP HANA.

With the right tools for the job, sometimes just as pilots to show return on investment, we can move on to the more interesting part of the work—achieving real business results.

Business Discovery

Business discovery is the critical step in transforming the unstructured mass of big data into actionable intelligence. The tools mentioned above enable companies to drill into the many levels of data, understand the connections among them, and open up new understanding and opportunities. They also take a complex, real-time, constantly evolving picture of a business and translate it into easily understood visuals. This process of business discovery enables businesses to see a new, more complete and more encompassing business model.

And, as technology develops and more data is created, the potential for generating actionable intelligence across more and more areas is set to grow.

Retailers, for example, can gather data from customer loyalty cards and link them to other data from their customers' social networks. Such intelligence will allow them to better understand who their customers are and their influence upon other existing or potential customers. Companies can then more effectively target their marketing and make better predictions of purchasing behavior.

Let us take another hypothetical example of actionable intelligence: A man is walking down the street in Singapore and he faints because his pacemaker has stopped. An ambulance is called to the scene.

A few minutes earlier a woman had tweeted about seeing a man who appeared dazed. Fifteen minutes before that security cameras had captured this man looking confused because the pacemaker was failing, and for the past few hours the pacemaker status had indicated failure. If all of that data had been correlated, the man's pacemaker malfunction could have been prevented. At the very least, the data would have enabled the ambulance drivers to get to the location earlier and react faster based on facts to improve the outcome for the man.

The scenario just described might sound far-fetched, but think about how what we take for granted today sounded equally far-fetched just a few years ago:

- Investors keeping track of thousands of stocks at once without the aid of a massive computer system, something we can now do on the move in the palm of our hands.
- Manufacturing companies able to view the real-time performance of every manufacturing line in every plant in every location around the world by computer. Today, this is expected in any enterprise resource planning (ERP) system.

What we considered big data 30 years ago is not complex and challenging now. Looking three decades into the future, today's big data will also be simple.

Improving Outcomes

The key to improving outcomes is the combination of tools, people, and processes—the "capability set" that allows us to capture and process this data to deliver actionable intelligence *in time* to improve business outcomes.

Speed is of the essence. Intelligence, after all, is only of real value if you receive it quickly enough to make use of it.

Already, next-generation leaders are leveraging big data and developing capabilities for delivering greater levels of actionable intelligence. By pulling in data from complex, high-volume sources like social media sentiment, customer movements tracked via cell phone apps, and real-time resource location, businesses can determine instantly what the optimum future outcome can be, improving the accuracy of business planning and overall corporate performance.

These capabilities enable companies to seize opportunities that others cannot. Meanwhile, companies that fail to leverage their own big data to extract actionable intelligence may miss out on potentially massive savings and could succumb to their competitors and current marketplace forces.

To take one recent example, industrial giant General Electric (GE) says it believes the utility industry can extract about $150 billion of unrealized efficiencies by using already existing data in smarter ways.

Using what it calls "immersive" data visualization, GE's Grid IQ software allows utility firms to better monitor their infrastructure, applying data streams to deliver intelligence that enables them to respond to business changes at high speed and, critically, in time to make a difference.

The message to any business is clear: Smart use of data to answer key questions about your business is essential to building a more encompassing business model and giving you the edge on your competitors.

Businesses that have yet to start developing actionable intelligence capabilities are at risk of becoming obsolete. Figure 1.3 illustrates the actionable intelligence goal companies should be reaching for.

So how can a company organize itself and what process should it follow to deliver actionable intelligence?

I recommend that businesses establish an actionable intelligence shared service group as shown in Figure 1.3 that reports into a senior leader in the business unit that needs the most performance improvement.

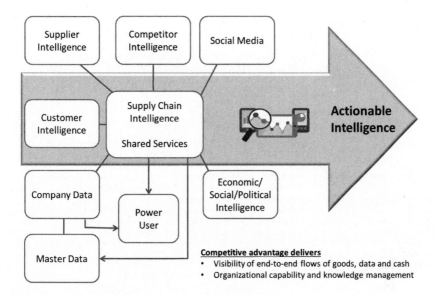

Figure 1.3   Actionable Intelligence from Big Data

At Estée Lauder, my department reported into the supply chain to try to reduce inventory and improve customer service. Your organization may need help in other areas, such as sales or marketing or finance. To determine which area to focus on, look at the departments that will likely have the highest chance of success. Choose the area with the following characteristics:

- Leaders have a vision for actionable intelligence.
- Critical business needs are clear, but the facts to improve the situation are lacking.
- There are resources and time to establish an organization to deliver the capabilities.

Businesses that have jumped onto the big data bandwagon without giving it much thought are finding themselves in a big mess. A 2012 study from International Data Corp. found that just 0.05 percent of available data in 2012 was analyzed. Gartner also estimates that, through 2015, 85 percent of the Fortune 500 companies will fail to exploit big data opportunities for a competitive advantage.

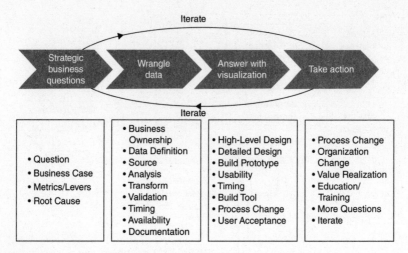

Figure 1.4   SWAT Iteration Framework

Business leaders around the world recognize the strategic edge that big data brings. At the recent Big Data World conference in Singapore, many of the executives that I spoke with see the value of big data, but they are not quite sure how to get there. Figure 1.4 provides a simple yet effective SWAT framework to help business leaders translate big data into actionable intelligence.

S—Strategic Business Questions   Every business has its priorities and overall strategy. As business leaders, it is important to understand that big data is intertwined with your overall strategy. Direct your big data efforts depending on the strategic priorities of your company. And, do not try to source all the data—focus just on the "burning platform." The strategic business question should be a guide.

This critical first step focuses the effort, gains sponsorship, and ensures the priority of the project remains high. The results at the end will also garner the right amount of visibility when the answers are delivered. After years of implementing business intelligence without tangible results, it's time to focus on the real business questions.

I was asked, "Do companies know the critical questions?" Emphatically, yes. There are common questions senior management asks including:

- How can we increase sales and customer service?
- Why do we have so much inventory?

- How can we reduce returns and quality issues?
- How can we increase profitable sales and net profit overall?
- Who are our customers and how can we answer their needs best?

Selecting one question to focus on allows for the rapid, iterative development to occur as the business and technology teams can focus. The narrative to describe the project becomes easier as well. Clarity of purpose allows sponsors and supporters to get behind the project because they'll clearly see the opportunity to deliver tangible results.

Comparatively, if the technology team is tasked with establishing a technology foundation for Big Data with the general reason to enable the business to answer these questions, the task can be so overwhelming to try to collect the data. Sponsors and supporters will be disappointed as usual as the project extends beyond the time when the answers were important.

Sponsors want quick results with low cost. This isn't possible unless the project is focused and purpose driven.

W—Wrangle Data   While many people have been advocating the mass collection of data, you should follow a different approach. The data needs to be focused solely on the strategic question. This enables the acquisition team to collect and review data quality. The quality of your insights is only as good as the quality of your data sets. So, before you head out to collect any data that you can lay your hands on, pause for a moment to consider the following:

- What kind of data do you really need to answer the strategic business questions?
- Where can you find it?
- What are the IT infrastructure, tools, and policies needed?
- Who are the people on your team with the required skillset to analyze the data?
- How can you do all these things in a cost-effective manner?

By focusing on the required data you'll have solid business sponsorship to access data which can normally be blocked by politics, siloed mentality, or lack of resources to gather the data. The difficulty of pulling together data from all parts of the organization, business units, and geographies can stop an Actionable Intelligence project in its tracks.

This work should be done with an rapid and iterative framework like this:

- A quick blast out to all parties to request the data
- Focus on working with those who provide positive responses and results
- Verify the data and if right incorporate into the data repository
- Repeat steps to gather more data

A—Answer with Visualization   According to Napoleon Bonaparte, "A good sketch is better than a long speech." Raw data displayed in Excel is difficult to use to garner insights. Fortunately, innovation in the field of data visualization has created business discovery tools that make things easier and more effective. For example, QlikTech (NASDAQ:QLIK) has created a tool called Qlikview that provides user-friendly yet concise executive dashboard and report capabilities.

However, while tools such as QlikView enable results, the process of developing a framework for that visualization is critical to success. Typical intelligence tools visualize data after you select a specific filter. But Qlikview goes the other way around. The data and relationships are all visible to you to discover new opportunities. You have to see the difference to believe it.

To gain the most benefits at this stage someone on the team needs to have a vision for how the answers will be used. For that vision to come alive you should hold regular (weekly or at least monthly) design sessions with business users, asking:

- How will the answer be used?
- How can we best show "Where We Are Today?"
- How can we show "How to Win Tomorrow"?
- How do we embed intelligence into the business?
- How will the standard operating procedures change?
- Are the right critical issues being highlighted for review?

T—Take Action   With a visual answer supported by good data, we move into the "take action" phase. Review the answer with the sponsor, and determine the actions to be taken in the short term and the long term, including:

- What actions can we take right now?
- Can we capture the value saved or earned?

- Does the current process and organization need to change to start making fact-based decisions?

Inevitably, the first answers will generate more and deeper questions. Start the SWAT framework again and quickly provide answers again . . . fast.

The SWAT framework enables fast, continuous delivery of actionable intelligence.

Take the following example: Imagine you work on the intelligence team of a company that manufactures toy cars in different shapes and sizes. Things were going great with your toys—the kids loved them. But, recently, kids have been more interested in tablet PCs than cars.

So, here's a new challenge to keeping the company profitable. The strategic question left unanswered is: Are we maximizing our profit?

One day, your boss asks you to visualize the revenues and costs of each business unit. Your team gathers the right revenue and cost data for each business unit. You then visualize that data to show how different business units are doing.

You show your visualization to your boss to answer his question. But your boss notices one unit—say, the toy fire truck department—performing particularly badly. He delves into the individual costs in his tool and discover where the money went. Apparently, the toy fire trucks cost double the manpower of toy police cars but are sold for the same price. Now your boss has some information that suggests all production should be switched to toy cars. But to get a full picture of whether he should do that, you might need to deliver more information about the product lines including:

- What is the historic demand for fire trucks and police cars?
- How is it changing?
- What social media chatter is going on about the products?
- Who is the customer and what are we doing to attract more of the same?

Now you've sparked something—a bit of actionable intelligence. Of course, the entire process is slightly more complicated.

Throughout this process there are some goals you should strive for. I call these goals the Vision of Actionable Intelligence:

- Easy-to-access internal and external information that enables decision makers at all levels to quickly answer questions with facts
- Good data quality (on time and accurate)

- Ability to access answers during meetings, walking down the hallway, on the way to the airport, or while talking to a customer without ever having to send an e-mail to a colleague in a different information silo

Actionable intelligence stands for more than just visualizing your data. It requires you to break down the silo structure of different departments and their data to equip the people in a company with the full picture of the situation.

Here is where the major ERP systems fall dramatically short. Companies rarely connect these systems to all internal and external functions, so the reports and data warehouses run short of the information needed to fully provide actionable intelligence.

In such an environment with data silos and shortfalls, users need to cobble together data from many different sources into some sort of spreadsheet. This situation is so common that I have found in speaking to large companies around the world that Microsoft Excel seems to be the most used tool for performing business analysis.

Indeed, in the fall of 2012, I spoke at a conference on end-to-end visibility and asked the 300-plus participants whether they use Excel along with a business intelligence (BI) tool to get a full picture of data. One hundred percent said yes.

When I asked how many use more than one BI tool, 90 percent said they did. So, big companies with big budgets—enough to pay $2,200 per head to attend a conference—still don't have a BI tool that meets their complete needs. Why?

In addition to breaking down silos, actionable intelligence creates massive benefits for companies—often bigger than you could even imagine.

Stages of Actionable Intelligence: Getting Ready for the Journey by Knowing Where You Are and Where to Go

Before you start off on your journey of actionable intelligence and big data, take a moment to assess where you on the maturity curve. (See Table 1.1.)

Table 1.1 Stages of Actionable Intelligence

Stage	Description	Visibility	Data Quality	Method of Collecting Data
No facts	• "I'm right! Believe me! Let me tell you." • "I know that this is going to work! I can feel it!" Individuals who rely on their gut feelings and make decisions based on feelings instead of facts	Backward looking	Unknown	Inconsistent
Invested, but no benefits yet	"IT will let us know." • Getting conned by the consultant • Stage of wasting a lot of money	Backward looking, but copies of manual reports are automated	Straight copies from unverified sources	Extract Transform Load (ETL)/slow
Local hero	"Let me show you."	Customized results making it easier to make business decisions	Attested to by power users	ETL and guerrilla acquisition for speed
Intelligence leader	Fact-based decision-making practitioner for strategic business questions • Here is my potential outcome. • This is the band of optimal outcome.	• Forward looking • Potential opportunities and risks • End-to-end visibility optimized	• Known catalogued • Data KPIs accompany senior management dashboards	Planned and executed with excellence

No Facts . . . So, Use Your Gut?

In the traditional decision making process, leaders rely on their gut feelings and their intuition to tell them what is right and where they should go. However, it is a backward-looking approach that reacts without any supporting evidence.

Despite the advances in technologies and a whole bookshelf of business intelligence tomes, some companies still choose to remain in this stage. According to an SAS Institute survey conducted among data management professionals, about 32 percent of the companies are in this stage.[1]

This could be because they tend to have a more traditional culture and they are resistant to change. Thus, it is not surprising that most of them are not the dominating market leaders or big players.

Invested Money and Time but Not Yet Receiving Tangible Benefits

Companies that are willing to take the first steps to overcoming resistance to change and start exploring the realm of intelligence may soon find themselves stuck in a situation where they are spending lots of money and feeling like they are not getting the most out of the engagement of their consultants. This is because improving the data quality and acquisition process will take significant time and effort. As such, most people who don't understand the proper sequence for incorporating intelligence into the culture will conclude their strategy is not working and will, thus, remain stuck in the situation. The SAS Institute survey shows that 39 percent of professionals who are exploring big data are in this stage.

Local Hero

Leaders who have maintained good-quality data in a central location, have worked with an extremely good consultant, or have read a good book about leveraging actionable intelligence and big data will probably find themselves at this stage—localized success. They have enjoyed quick wins that are impressive enough to convince top management or the rest of the team to sponsor the exploration of the project. According to the SAS survey, 16 percent of data management professionals are at this stage.

Intelligence Leader (Enterprise Actionable intelligence Capabilities)

With more funds, resources, and support from the rest of the team—coupled with the right combination of governance and cultural management—companies will join the 12 percent that are implementing/executing decisions based on big data. They will develop into fact-based enterprises that grow further and fly higher with actionable intelligence.

At which of these stages in Table 1.1 are you?

If we look at things from the "people" perspective, we can see some of the underlying factors that influenced the results of the projects. When people rely on gut feelings, they doubt their capabilities to adopt learning and adopt intelligence into their work and businesses. There are no key performance indicators (KPIs) to do it, and they generally feel apprehensive about taking the first step and try to find excuses to delay discussion or just to change the topic.

When they have overcome that fear and become beginners, they will start off with IT-led projects and IT-created KPIs. As the company starts to get more comfortable and confident about the projects, it will become "business-engaged," whereby business executives start to use intelligence on their own instead of demanding IT spoon-feed them the reports and information they require. They will also start to create business KPIs.

By the time the project reaches the stage shown in Table 1.1 of "local hero," the business would have taken control of the project and the project becomes business-led. Team members start to focus on and commit themselves to answering the strategic business questions and go deeper to try to gather the answers. When the process is done right and the savings are measured, people's capabilities reach the stage whereby they can deliver business results.

As the entire company buys into the new system, employees' lives are made easier and the benefits start rolling into the fact-based enterprise; leaders become apostles who spread the power of actionable intelligence to everyone. This is the stage you want to be in—and the stage you want to sustain yourself in.

Growing People's Capabilities on Actionable Intelligence

It's up to you to determine where you are and where you want to go. Table 1.2 provides descriptions of what actionable intelligence looks like

Table 1.2 Profiles in Actionable Intelligence

Profile	Description	Measuring Results
No leadership	• "I don't know what analytics is." • "Intelligence = 007?" • "It's impossible for us to do it."	No KPIs. Projects completed but original business case not reviewed.
Information Technology(IT)-led	"Hey IT, just run the report for us."	IT created KPIs that don't quite fit the business needs.
Business engaged	"I'll create the report myself."	Business created KPIs.
Business led	"Let's focus on the strategic business questions."	Go deeper to retrieve.
Business results	"I've delivered results with forward intelligence."	Act and shine.
Apostles	"Everyone should know the power of actionable intelligence."	Shares results with others.

in different companies and how it's measured. You are already equipped with the roadmap and an idea, a vision of what actionable intelligence should look like for you. Time to start!

Are You Ready to Take the First Step?

In this chapter, we have seen what actionable intelligence can lead to and the world of change it creates. In the next four chapters, different steps in the process to create your own actionable intelligence program will be highlighted. All business, nothing too technical. With the help of this book you can become the next Zhuge Liang, a sage who delivers limitless value to your organization, enabling your organization to see a 360-degree view of the situation and be proactive in decision making.

It does not matter what function you perform in an organization or what kind of organization you work in. You will have the power to inspire, define a vision, and rally followers to share your beliefs. You will have the power to empower coworkers and give them actionable intelligence.

Why Is It Called Actionable Intelligence and Not Analytics or Big Data?

The words we use create feelings and pictures in our mind. It is really important to use words that provide an instant response in our audience.

For example, Bond . . . James Bond versus analyst.

Or just take the word analytics apart into its syllables and you arrive at unfortunate primary school jokes. If you are the head of analytics well, I'd change that if I were you . . . just saying. Or at a loud cocktail party try shouting, "I'm into analytics!"

Seriously, let's look at each phrase.

Big data. No one heard about it till a year ago; geeks, tech sales, and technical marketing loved it; it sounds so smart, but what does it mean to the rest of the world? Recently, I asked an audience of 150 people and five panelists at a conference on big data to define it. The panelists had six different definitions and the audience wasn't sure at all. We do not have any reference to it from growing up. It means nothing except how pundits are trying to define it.

In my view big data is a state, a situation, that defines a set of data that no one is using and may not know how to use. Thousands of years ago when the Romans did a census, they wrote down a lot of information but had no easy way to process it. Compared to today, a census is easily viewed, visualized, and used to make decisions using computers. What was big data in the Roman era is now just . . . data. Today, companies have data about their products from social media and millions of transactions in myriad interconnected systems. When a company cannot leverage this data into information to make decisions, we can call it big data.

According to Merriam-Webster, analytics is defined as: the method of logical analysis.[2]

So what is analysis? Again, Merriam-Webster's definition:[3]

1: separation of a whole into its component parts

2 a: the identification or separation of ingredients of a substance; **b:** a statement of the constituents of a mixture

3 a: proof of a mathematical proposition by assuming the result and deducing a valid statement by a series of reversible steps; **b** (1): a branch of mathematics concerned mainly with limits, continuity, and infinite series (2): calculus 1b

4 a: an examination of a complex, its elements, and their relations; **b:** a statement of such an analysis

5 a: a method in philosophy of resolving complex expressions into simpler or more basic ones; **b:** clarification of an expression by an elucidation of its use in discourse

Do we have all year to create a discourse on the opportunities we need to seize because our competitor stumbled or a new trend just emerged? No. Businesses need to be agile, responsive, and when a customer comes yelling, "Where's my stuff?" we can't turn to our helpful discourse on analytics. Nor would it help in the exceptional cases when the "stuff" went missing or had a quality problem or the government of XYZ country just collapsed. After all, those events were not in the model.

Actionable Intelligence: Merriam Webster's definition of both words:

Actionable: synonyms: useful, applicable, functional, usable, workable.[4]

Here's the definition:

1: subject to or affording ground for an action or suit at law
2: capable of being acted on <actionable information>

Intelligence definition (*Merriam-Webster Dictionary,* 2014):

1a (1): the ability to learn or understand or to deal with new or trying situations: reason; also: the skilled use of reason (2): the ability to apply knowledge to manipulate one's environment or to think abstractly as measured by objective criteria (as tests)

2a: information, news; **b:** information concerning an enemy or possible enemy or an area; also: an agency engaged in obtaining such information

Now, we can see by definition that actionable intelligence is the right phrase for business. Do not follow the crowd and use what the pundits are saying; it simply does not apply to business. This book is about taking action, being practical, and being smart! Enable your organization with actionable intelligence capabilities, and you will win again and again.

And one more thing: Figure 1.5 provides some statistics to get you excited. Industries of all type are gaining from leveraging big data into actionable intelligence to achieve better results in sales and cost reductions.

Benefits of Effective Data

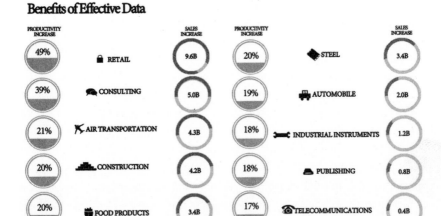

Figure 1.5 Benefits of Effective Data
SOURCE: "Business Benefits of Effective Data" from University of Austin study, 2010.

Summary and Considerations

Point to Ponder: Define the vision, make it great!

Quote to Remember: "As the entire company buys into the new system, employees' lives are made easier and the benefits start rolling into the fact-based enterprise; leaders become apostles who spread the power of actionable intelligence to everyone. This is the stage you want to be in—and the stage you want to sustain yourself in."

Question to Consider: What is the question our organization is passionate about, and is there interest in answering it?

Notes

1. 2013 Big Data Survey Research Brief, www.sas.com/resources/whitepaper/wp_58466.pdf.
2. *Merriam-Webster Dictionary*, an Encyclopedia Britannica Company, www.merriam-webster.com/dictionary/analytics.
3. Ibid., www.merriam-webster.com/dictionary/analysis.
4. Ibid., www.merriam-webster.com/dictionary/actionable.

Chapter 2

Discovery of the Business Situation (Business Discovery)

Key Points and Questions

- Answer sponsored strategic questions all the time.
- Taking too long to answer a question results in lost opportunities.
- Good business leaders ask questions so they can guide their business to become great.
- Great business leaders prioritize their questions and dedicate resources to find the answers. They create and sustain the capabilities to make fact-based decisions.

In the late 1400s, wars and bandits around the key trade routes through the Middle East to Asia made it difficult for the Europeans to travel to India and China. Christopher Columbus believed there was a shorter route to Asia that could be found by traveling in the opposite direction. In order to prove his great theory, he set off in search of sponsors and support. He took his plans to the kings of Portugal, Genoa, and Venice. He was rejected by all. He even asked his brother to seek an audience with Henry VII of England, but to no avail.

In 1486, when he went to the Spanish monarchy of Isabella of Castille and Ferdinand of Aragon, they were skeptical about his ideas. However, they saw the potential in Christopher Columbus and wanted to keep their options open. They kept him on a retainer with monthly allowances to prevent him from taking his plans to others.

When the Spanish army finally took over the last Muslim stronghold in Granada in January 1492, Christopher Columbus was finally given the opportunity he had been waiting for: The Spanish monarchs agreed to sponsor his voyage. In August 1492, Columbus left Spain (headed, despite what he thought, for the "New World").

The Spanish monarchs financed the voyage of Christopher Columbus and his crew with the expectation of finding a new way to trade and new partners to trade with. If anyone had told them the return on their investment would be a new continent, gold, oil, and other bountiful natural resources, they wouldn't have believed it. In fact, the Spanish monarchs did not even expect Columbus to return.

Today, companies have a new world of data they need to discover. They need to understand the value of their data inside their four walls and the big data outside. To do so requires going on a voyage—a voyage of business discovery.

However, most companies have not even attempted this venture because:

- They do not have exploratory talent like Columbus and his small crew.
- They cannot fully envision the benefits.
- Politically, it is not typically the "good-old boy" who can deliver this but an aggressive outsider who can get past the politics and positioning to achieve the results.

And it is not even just businesses—or Spanish monarchies—that can benefit from this voyage of discovery. Most any organization can.

A friend who teaches public elementary school in Massachusetts shared with me that the drive toward data-driven education sometimes ignores the fact that data is being collected about humans—young humans. And what incents and dis-incents these humans may have nothing or everything to do with the material being taught and assessed.

For example, my teacher friend had a student who scored poorly on the state's standardized math and English language arts tests. The teacher and other staff pored over the data from the tests and other instruments to try to determine the best way to close the gap in this child's learning. What the data did not show, however, was that the student was going through a very difficult time at home. The best material and most focused instruction would not help this student learn because—it was discovered—he did not feel safe at home. The latter needed to be taken care of before the former could even be attempted.

When you think about it, teaching and learning are all about big data, and, indeed, education is moving toward a data-driven model. When a teacher gets a new classroom of students, he or she can read each student's records, examine past standardized test scores, and review work samples.

But the picture that the data draws is not really clear at all—at least, it is not complete.

"Ultimately, student achievement data alone only yield a 'black box,'" noted Frederick M. Hess, author of *Common Sense School Reform*, in an article published in *Educational Leadership* magazine. "They illustrate how students are faring but do not enable an organization to diagnose problems or manage improvement. It is as if a CEO's management dashboard consisted of only one item—the company stock's price."[1]

Indeed, teachers have to explore further—go on a voyage of discovery. For example, do low standardized test scores reflect a low academic ability, or do they reflect the fact that the student's father lost his job, that his mother is working the second shift and so isn't home when the student gets off the bus, and that the student was hungry the morning of the standardized assessment?

A teacher who looks only at quantitative data—with little or no regard for the human being who is behind the data—will never fully realize the benefits that new teaching practices or units of study will uncover. The teacher needs to go on a voyage of discovery—he or she needs to speak to the student's family, his friends, past teachers, the administration, and—of course—the student himself.

Only then will the teacher begin to see and truly understand the student. The teacher can try new teaching techniques and present material in different ways. The teacher may find that the student is able to effectively demonstrate understanding not in conventional ways but through drawing and play-acting.

In this example, the teacher is able to understand the value of the data within the four walls of the school but is willing to go beyond that data to get to benefits as yet unknown.

Normal assessment of students is significantly overweighted with one factor: performance on continuous assessment. Arguably, this can assess the student's ability in several areas: memorization of facts and methods, logic, reasoning, and ability to perform under time pressure. But to understand how a student may perform in arts, science, and engineering, how do we assess their ability to visualize, innovate, inspire, and perspire? Wouldn't it be wonderful if for primary school students we could:

- Match students who learn better with hands-on and practical work with teachers that provide that experience
- Create classes and exams that cater to students "on-the-move" versus those who can sit for two hours quietly writing away
- Assess the parents' ability to provide a nurturing environment and teach them their role in education

The common theme across these three ideas is having actionable intelligence on our students to enable them to excel in learning. The strategic business question is, "How we prepare the next generation to improve the economic output of a nation."

By acquiring data on the student's, teacher's, and parents' teaching and study habits we can visualize the right matrix of factors that will drive success. As long as we can act on the findings, we will be able to deliver better learning outcomes.

What can you do for those in your life who are learning to achieve a better outcome?

Government Intelligence

In 2009, I happened to need to visit the Singapore Embassy in Washington, D.C., for a dinner hosted by the past ambassador Chan Heng Chee. My family and I drove down from New York and had a fantastic time as usual. We stayed overnight, and, during the drive back home, I saw a sign for The National Cryptologic Museum located at the National Security Agency campus.

Curious, I took the entire family on a detour. We passed the National Security Agency (NSA) building and lots of odd, space-age buildings jutting out of the ground here and there. Were they complex listening and collection devices? Who knows? I was just excited about seeing the NSA and the Cryptologic Museum.

Once inside the latter, we saw the famous red phone of presidents, encryption machines, and the Hall of Intelligence Heroes: the men and women who broke codes, deciphered communications, and changed the course of history by providing actionable intelligence at the speed the government and military required.

I was so inspired by that trip; top-performing governments have efficient information acquisition and management structures. When information is placed into the hands of the right people, the right actions happen, often just in time to save lives or protect interests.

The National Security Agency has example after example of providing actionable intelligence to visionary decision makers—in enough time to prevent catastrophes. The means and methods and depth of information may be concerning, but the fact is that to protect against future threats we need to dig into the data share. (The biggest problem now is that with the exposure of Eric Snowden by the media, the bad guys know more about what to do to avoid detection.)

The Finnish have a word, "aavistus." In the United States, we call it intuition. Many businesses have intuition about risks and opportunities, but it can be too time-consuming or expensive to collect all the data necessary to gel the intuition into fact-based decisions.

This is the dilemma that many professionals face today: They might have the right ideas and intuition, but there is not enough financial support or resources to get to real and true answers. However, this should not be a deterring factor for you—not just yet. Do some research to find out the challenges you need to overcome and what you are in for.

For my first intelligence project, we had to deliver intelligence quickly but had zero budget and very little manpower. So I did some research as to what we should expect to achieve and how to get there—much like you are doing now.

A great place to start is a book by Jeanne Harris and Thomas Davenport, *Competing on Analytics: The New Science of Winning.*[2] The book details many examples of how companies used analytics to beat their competitors. The commonality among these companies lies in how they were able to better connect with their customers.

For example:

- Netflix uses the previous selections of its users to suggest the movies they might like to watch in the future. This allows customers to feel they can get more out of their services because when new movies come out, they will know what to watch. For the company, a higher success rate of suggesting movies to the customer translates into higher customer satisfaction and higher ratings. This, in turn, leads to more customer references and recommendations. The data was always there (sales receipts of purchases online).
- Another example of a company that has successfully used intelligence is 1–800-Flowers. It built an online flower business that essentially replaced FTD. 1–800-Flowers got to know its customers very well. As a result, the customer gets good service and good products at a good price.
- Will Smith, the actor, uses analytics to decide what movies he will star in. He looks at the genre, the story arc, the ending, and the role he will play. He then analyzes similar movies to see what their box office performance has been. Then he selects the role carefully based on the data.

It all starts with the strategic question. Before you get to the detailed answers with analytics, you need to have a culture of storytelling. The most successful companies train people to tell stories about their data. They are able to look at a set of data, see the relationships between the data and business problems, and then relate to senior management the current situation, opportunities, and threats, and recommended actions based on the facts.

But after reading this book I was left with many questions:

- How did all those companies and Will Smith actually deliver these dreamlike capabilities?
- What was actually improved, and how much was monetized?
- What was the business case for hiring and training analysts?

- What was the business case for data management?
- How could we deliver these capabilities fast, and what would governance look like?

Ask the Questions

Business decisions are based on questions about the current situation and how that situation can be improved. Those are called strategic business questions. It can be tempting to execute business decisions without as full and fact-based an answer as one would like when the data is hard to acquire, or when the team is becoming exhausted by trying to put together a story. It is a race to deliver answers before:

- The question has changed or moved on.
- The priority to answer the question has been reduced.
- The opportunity to answer is gone.

At a chief financial officers (CFO) roundtable I asked, "What's stopping you from delivering actionable intelligence?"

One CFO said passionately, "I have enough data, but my people can't give me *answers!*"

All executives need to ask, "Can I, today, afford to be lacking as much visual information as I need to answer my most pertinent questions?"

There is only one answer: "No."

Your competitors may already have the capability to answer their most important questions. Even if they do not, the marketplace is changing. Without this capability, your business may not perform as well as it could. Your business might end up in the emergency room simply by making a seemingly small wrong decision or by not taking timely action.

When you have a business question that is important enough to spend money answering, you start off gathering the data that makes sense to answer the question.

One tip, however: Control your scope/control the investment. You do not have to gather data from around the whole world. You do not have to build a huge vault, nor invest in all sorts of computing power-scaling analysis right off the bat. You just need the precise data necessary to answer your question.

Controlling scope and working from strategic business questions will be a central theme throughout the discussion of implementing actionable intelligence.

Answer the Questions: Business Discovery

The crucial step that follows asking questions is—you guessed it— answering the questions. That is what the efforts of gathering data and creating actionable intelligence capabilities will be all about. By answering people's (leadership-sponsored) strategic business questions as well as possible with the available data and compelling visualizations, you can obtain the money and buy-in to grow your efforts, grow your team, and develop the project.

However, what strikes me as odd is that this seemingly simple and iterative pattern of asking a question and getting an answer is often not supported by traditional business intelligence (BI) tools.

Traditional BI tools operate by answering a predetermined set of questions. In this model, IT also plays a large role in churning out the fixed reports for the rest of the business.

In contrast, there is a movement to create a set of tools allowing a free-roam approach to answering questions in which answers can be created on the go by combining any type of data that's already available in a user-friendly visualization. This approach is more user-driven and allows users to create questions while they are digging in the data and explore the data for the right answer.

Gartner calls this approach "data discovery," and QlikView, a key proponent of this type of BI, calls it "business discovery." The discovery part lies in the opportunity for users to discover new facts in existing data and to discover new questions while exploring the data.

Here is QlikView's definition of business discovery (see Figure 2.1):

Business Discovery is a whole new way of answering questions that puts the business user in control. Unlike traditional BI, where just a few people are involved in insight creation, Business Discovery enables everyone to create insight. It's about work-groups, departments, and entire business units having access to the data they need to make better decisions."[3]

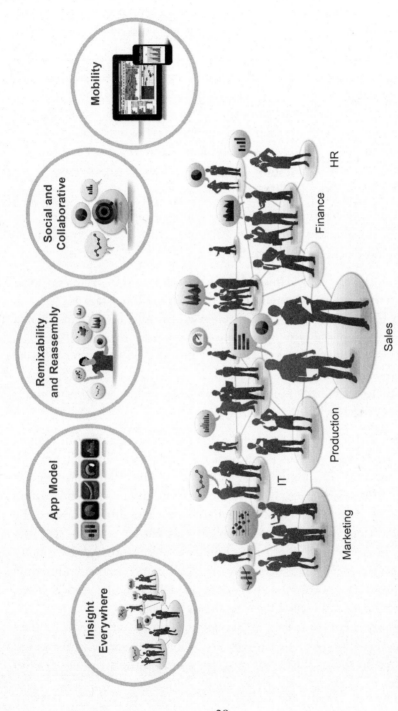

Figure 2.1 QlikView Business Discovery Ecosystem

SOURCE: Illustration by QlikTech, Inc.

In my article published in NUS (National University of Singapore) *Think Business* magazine (June 3, 2013) called "Big Data: What's the Big Deal?," I go further to define business discovery as:

> Taking a complex, real-time, constantly evolving picture of a business and translating it into easily understood visuals, these tools enable us to drill into the many levels of data, understand the connections between them and open up new understanding and opportunities. This process of "business discovery" enables businesses to see a new, more complete and more encompassing business model.

I would never say a company has a lack of reports, but, rather, it is typically missing the right analytical tools. During business discovery you should be asking questions like:

- Do I have the critical business information I need to make decisions?
- Are the data management teams maintaining the data well?
- To review historical versus present and future, is my data aligned between my old systems and any new systems?
- Are my people trained and capable of using the intelligence to make better decisions?
- Is there a feedback loop that allows us to show we are using intelligence the right way?

I believe business leaders need ready answers to their business questions. Knowing the status of business can't be a monthly exercise with data from weeks or months in the past. It should be consumable enough to be a daily or weekly exercise with a view into future possibilities based on current plans. Preferably, some modeling or multiple plans can be looked at to see what happens in various scenarios.

Leaders also need to provide visibility to their teams. With visibility, the team can make better decisions; team members can spend more time executing on opportunities they see instead of spending critical hours collecting data and formatting a report in Excel.

Energy spent on collating data detracts significantly from the time and energy of analysis. That is why actionable intelligence is the logical next step in the evolution of efficiency mechanisms for any type of business.

Business Discovery Example

Let me give an example of business discovery at Estee Lauder, my previous employer.

When I wanted to know why the customer service level was low and what level it could be at in the future, my team and I considered what we needed to know. First, we needed to ask the question: "What is customer service?" We determined that it is orders from our customers, with the products shipped on time and in full, of good quality, and with all the right paperwork. In addition, we needed to understand and be able to measure customer service performance. To do so, we considered what we would need to measure for the achievement of the "perfect order":

- Customer information and the order information
- Inventory and forecast
- Information on the items/services
- Segmentation information such as brands and category

I directed my intelligence team to focus on the heart of the strategic business questions to visualize a fast answer.

Our strategic questions were:

- How can we improve our customer service?
- How can we avoid inventory mistakes?
- How can we make sustainable changes in our supply chain?

As soon as we started to delve into these questions, we realized there was a vast amount of data in a collection of BI reports, Microsoft Access databases, Excel files and other systems. We knew we needed to focus on the data relevant to the question, or we'd be lost in a soupy sea of information.

We needed to go deeper. We needed to align our discovery with our business goals:

- Where are we in terms of our business performance? This applies to our strategy, tactics, and where we wanted to go as a business.
- What do we need to try to do to become more competitive?

Each business will have its own set of strategic business questions. Your company might be fine in these areas; you might instead be looking at quality or purchasing improvements. To be sure, every company has opportunities to make more fact-based decisions.

To succeed, we needed to prioritize the strategic business questions, set expectations on the delivery date of the answers, and then deliver in small steps following an iterative business discovery model.

With regard to prioritizing, always remember the following:

- Good business leaders ask questions so they can guide their business better.
- Great business leaders prioritize their questions and dedicate resources to find the answers. They create and sustain the capabilities to make fact-based decisions.

Business leaders give direction to the company and its strategy, but they also give direction to the business discovery process. So, to put together an effective apparatus to disseminate data and answer questions, you need to find the answers to the most important questions. This will help you start up the effort to provide real answers for everyone's big questions. On top of that, you have the opportunity to attract sponsors to your cause—a victory whose importance should never be underestimated.

And whatever the development, don't stop focusing on the core: answering sponsored business questions.

One caveat. You simply cannot answer every important question. There will be a limit to what you can and cannot do, especially in terms of budget, manpower, and expertise. To demonstrate your new capabilities, it's important to figure out what business questions can be answered well—without straining resources to such an extent that it will hamper your results.

At Estée Lauder, we first tackled the global inventory tool, which allowed us to gather the inventories of Estée Lauder, centralize them, and pick up on the details, for example, location, price, and SKU number.

Visual Consistency and the First Tool

We brought in a team, the MLH Group, that is very good at visualizing the strategic business questions in QlikView. Helena May and her team brought a deep knowledge of data models and visualization, without which we couldn't make the information come to life.

When you use an Apple product, your experience includes consistency, ease of use, smoothness of interaction, and fit/finish. Each tool we created was built to meet the "Apple standard" of user experience. Keep in mind: We weren't IT, so we actually had to use these tools to do work when we were done creating them. It was in our best interest to make the tools easy, fast, and effective.

NOTE

The business and IT have different motivations. The project budget is used to deliver functions, not ease-of-use. Business users want ease of delivering results post go-live.

Even if IT is on the hook for results, they do not have to use the tools they build, so the incentive to achieve Apple-like simplicity, which is very complex to attain, is not there for IT. Unless the business doesn't allow go-live until simplicity and ease-of-use are achieved, it will get tools that are complicated to use.

Gaining Support with Our First Tool: Global Inventory Tool

Harry Bennett, former head of quality assurance for Estee Lauder's North American operations, is a long-time mentor and friend. When I first started working at Estée Lauder, we met and he took me through the intelligence capabilities he had provided to the packaging and quality assurance (QA) teams. It was the year 2000, and he had broken down silos to gather data into Microsoft Access to provide visibility to projects. His passion and enthusiasm for data have always been impressive. In 2010, it made sense to me to show him the new actionable intelligence tool first.

I met him at his office on a high floor in the General Motors building. After we caught up a bit, I drew Harry's attention to his computer screen and asked him to open the global inventory tool on our internal QlikView server.

I showed him how the About tab provided documentation on how to use the tool and, importantly, all the acronyms related to inventory so new people could understand the business terms. We then jumped right into the Global Inventory tab. I showed him how we could filter on all types of metadata and search. I turned to Harry and asked, "Is there an item that has a QA issue that you are concerned about right now?"

He thought for a moment, and noted that there was a product that was interacting with packaging the wrong way.

After he gave me the product name, voilà! Instantly, he was able to see the locations of the inventory in manufacturing, distribution, in transit, and at our sales affiliates with information that was just refreshed that morning.

He saw that he could quickly drill into the results to see inventory details like quality status, expiration date, value, categorization, and so forth.

I asked him how long it would normally take him to find this information, and he answered that it would normally take three to four days—and that's if he had all of the correct information.

I asked if he would support me in showing the global inventory tool to the Supply Chain Leadership Team (SCLT). He said yes, but suggested we show it first to Pat Chiappetta, former VP of Global Quality Assurance at the Estee Lauder Companies, Inc.

We visited Pat, who welcomed Harry and me, and I demonstrated the capabilities again.

One of the key benefits of this tool was the ability it afforded us to see the quality assurance status in each location around the world. The QA team was able to reduce the products on QA hold from $24 million to $6 million globally. The benefits included converting inventory into sales, clearing up space in our distribution centers, avoiding the manufacturing of additional products, and more.

Next, I provided a demonstration to the SCLT in the hopes of bolstering support for our work. Note that we were not provided additional budget for this work.

Little did I expect that there would be dissatisfaction! It came from one of the SCLT members, who claimed he hadn't been asked what capability he'd want for his department. In truth, I had identified him as an early potential stakeholder, but when I went to set up a time to meet with him, he pushed me off to one of his subordinates, who never followed through. It wasn't until much later that this department's capability would start to be developed, long after other departments were reaping the benefits.

The lesson I learned from this is that it is important to build support for your cause before going into a group meeting. Thankfully, I already had support and requirements from other parts of the business. If I hadn't, this one squeaky wheel might have delayed our project.

Off to the Races

Now you have seen how to discover and prioritize strategic business questions, the starting point in your journey, but we're not there yet. The questions are just the theoretical foundation, the justification for your project. What you need now is a practical foundation, something tangible, to go alongside the questions. To reach a satisfying answer you need something to base that answer on. You need data. And not just any data—you need the right data. It's a race, but don't make it a rat race.

Summary and Considerations

Point to Ponder: Think it! Start it! Show it!
Quote to Remember: "You simply cannot answer every important question. There will be a limit to what you can and cannot do, especially in terms of budget, manpower, and expertise."
Question to Consider: What opportunities could you be seizing if you had forward-looking actionable intelligence capabilities right now?

Notes

1. Frederick M. Hess, "Data: Now What?" *Educational Leadership* (December 2008): 12-17.
2. Harvard Business Press, 2007.
3. QlikView Business Discovery as of February 14, 2013.

Chapter 3

Creating a Foundation of Data

Key Points and Questions

- Staying focused on the strategic business question is critical for the data acquisition process.
- Data accuracy and timeliness are critical to the success of delivering intelligence.
- How useful is your data? Do you have data quality reporting?
- "And Moses sent them to spy out the land of Canaan"

Information acquisition has a long history. In biblical times, there was already a dire need for the right information. Take the story of Joshua and Caleb and the 12 spies in Canaan. For those unfamiliar with the Bible, the short story is this:

The Israelites were just exiled from Egypt and were traveling to the Promised Land of Canaan. God promised the Israelites through their leader Moses that the land of Canaan would be a land of milk and honey in abundance, but they had to take it over from the current

47

inhabitants. Moses wanted actionable intelligence, full information about internal and external factors about the land and its people. He said, "Go up through the Negev and on into the hill country. See what the land is like and whether the people who live there are strong or weak, few or many. What kind of land do they live in? Is it good or bad? What kind of towns do they live in? Are they unwalled or fortified? How is the soil? Is it fertile or poor? Are there trees in it or not? Do your best to bring back some of the fruit of the land." (It was the season for the first ripe grapes.)

Twelve spies went out and traveled all over the lands of Canaan, which were very suitable for living, compared to the desert the Israelites were residing in at the time. In Canaan, the clusters of grapes were too big for one person to carry. The people living there were big and strong, and the towns were fortified with walls, but they had to make a decision.

So after 40 days of gathering intelligence on the enemy, the band of spies returned to where the Israelites were camping and told them of all the obstacles standing in the way of their claiming the land of Canaan. The Israelites were dismayed by the news. Some began questioning Moses' plans to enter the Promised Land at all, afraid they would be killed in battle. Only Joshua and Caleb tried to convince the others that although the people in the land were strong, it was the time to seize the opportunity.

And so by overanalyzing—by not following actionable intelligence but instead following their guts—the Israelites turned away from Canaan and started a 40-year journey of wandering across the desert. During the journey, all of the spies except Joshua and Caleb perished. Even Moses died just prior to reaching the Promised Land again. And under the reign of Joshua, Moses' successor, Canaan, was eventually taken.

The moral of this story: Bad things happen when people receive intelligence but act on their gut and hearsay instead of being guided by the facts.

Businesses also need timely access to facts to make the right decisions to enable them to grow faster, as opposed to being stuck in the desert of rumor, hearsay, and gut-based decisions. And to get facts we need a foundation to build on.

Building the Foundation

When building a house, you need to build a foundation. It is not beautiful, you cannot cost-justify it, and it is not even visible when the house is complete. Few house owners receive the praise, "What a nice foundation you have!"

This foundation building is not a new concept. Thousands of years ago a story was written about two men who each built his own house. One man built his beautiful house on sand. The other man took time to build a solid foundation for his house on rock. When the storms of change and challenge came, only the house built on solid rock was left standing.

In the same way, it can be tempting to just go and create the dashboard or rush to buy a business intelligence (BI) system instead of taking time to develop a strong foundation of a data dictionary and central repository. This temptation to immediately deliver visible results can hamper efforts to deliver significant, sustainable, measurable results. Neglecting the found-ation results in a chorus of "told you so," when, in the end, the business receives the same old reports with marginally better graphics. The weak foundational issues of missing or incorrect data still are not fixed.

What companies need to do instead is create a data dictionary that maps data names and definitions throughout the enterprise, and they need to validate the information. Documentation and validation are the solid rock foundation needed for actionable intelligence.

Benefits of Having the Right Data

What is the value of ensuring the data is correct?

Well, if the data is wrong you could miss shipments, disappoint cus-tomers, and possibly spend thousands of dollars reworking quality issues. Just avoiding one mistake pays for fixing this situation and also improves morale in the organization because employees can see where the problems are coming from and stop performing mind-numbing "checking" work.

A good tip would be to take the time to estimate the cost of past mistakes. Doing so should result in data management getting the atten-tion it deserves. Consider the following example:

- **A shipment to Thailand of . . .** *women?*
- The global supply chain team at a large cosmetics company received a message from the Thai authorities, "Your shipment has been held in customs because the documentation says the product is women."
- Imagine a shipping container being inspected. The company is ship-ping a full line of cosmetics to the Thai market to be sold in high-end retail stores: lush red lipsticks, sweet perfumes, luxurious accessories. The container was sent to replenish store inventories and launch a

new product. Now, the whole shipment is stuck in customs because of one small problem. The new product had not been named correctly in the system. Someone forgot to change from the working name to the real product name. For more than two weeks the container sat in the hot sun of Thailand's busiest port. The products won't get to the stores on time unless extraordinary, and expensive, efforts are made.

- The point is, data accuracy has real business implications. A simple data-entry flub cost thousands of dollars and delayed a shipment of new products to retail stores by several weeks—just one piece of data!

The Data Challenge

Notes Donald Farmer, VP, product management at QlikView: "People don't trust data. People trust other people and their opinion of the data."

It is easy to understand why. In a large corporation with more than 600 systems, lots of data, and no data quality dashboards, the strongest opinions of a few people reign supreme.

Explanations for poor customer service or projections for what it could be in the future are pure conjecture but, when stated with authority, are taken as fact.

More than one supply chain executive has implemented inventory optimizers, supply network planning, and other capabilities, only to find their organizations do not trust the output of these optimizers due to incomplete or incorrect data.

How can an inventory optimizer work in an environment where global inventory is not readily available? The answer is, it can't.

The challenge now is: How can we make people trust the data again?

The simple answer would be: Create a data foundation for the data in the company that is complete and accurate at all times.

However, it is impractical from the standpoint of time, resources, and fast delivery to try to create a data foundation of all data in a company. The strategic business questions need to be a guide for where to start and end. We need to find, acquire, and disseminate the data needed to answer the specific questions we need answered. Remember, focus on the questions at hand and work as efficiently as possible to assure success.

Acquire Data in Four Consistent Steps

When gathering data, the main thing to keep in mind is what the data will be used for. By constantly asking that question you can assure that you will not do unnecessary work when creating the foundation on which to build your successes. Ask yourself where the data will fit in the big picture. This will also let you make sure that you can answer your strategic business questions.

When you have figured out what strategic business questions you need to answer, it's time to create the foundation. Here, are the four steps you should take when creating the data foundation for actionable intelligence. Each step will be explained in detail.

Step 1: Identify the data needed and gather data from the known sources.

Step 2: Document the acquisition process into the data dictionary.

Step 3: Determine the data owners, validate the data with them, and create a data dashboard for those owners.

Step 4: Implement changes in people, processes, and systems to improve data quality.

Step 1: Identify the Data Needed and Gather Data from the Known Sources

If I am trying to decide what type of shoes to buy, I need to know what the weather looks like in the place I live. If I've slipped a couple of times on railroad platforms or steps on rainy days and I'm smart, then I also need to determine whether those incidents will be a factor in the shoes I decide to buy. I know whether I want comfortably tight or loose shoes. Do I need the shoes to be seen, and who will see them? How long will they need to last, given my budget? With all of this data collected, I then need to figure out where I can buy shoes. How can I collect them? So, I have focused my data collection on an internal set of data and an external set of data. If I only have the weekend to decide, I will become even more precise about the data I need to collect. In other words, I may not be able to collect all types of data.

Applying this principle to the business, after you have a sponsored business question, you need to make sure to start off with a list of the data you need to answer the question. With the question in mind, hold some ideation sessions and list key facts needed to answer the question and determine what is redundant. Go through a couple of rounds to figure out what those are. Then seek out the source of that data. Understand where it resides, how often it's updated, and how to access it.

Step 1 is perhaps the most straightforward: Identify the data you need, and place all the data in one place for you to use. Though that doesn't sound very complicated, it can take up most of your data collection process. This process takes weeks and months of approvals, requiring reviews by interested and not-so-interested parties (with a risk of a "no" or simply running out of time). That is the risk when working with people who have to give up control over their own data in exchange for the benefits of actionable intelligence.

It is possible that the process of gathering your most important data will be so exhausting and costly that the project of creating actionable intelligence will never get past this stage. That is why it is very important to gather only the data that is necessary for the business questions at hand. You can always collect additional data down the line.

It might be helpful to set up a (temporary) data repository to centralize and control the data you are going to use, making quick connections to all the data you need at different sources. The IT department can be of great help in setting up a server to get that data repository up and running. In fact, never underestimate the help a good IT department can offer—if it is convinced that a plan has merit and can actually work.

Step 2: Document the Acquisition Process into the Data Dictionary

To start your data acquisition, typically you need some smart computer person to go and tap into the data source. This person can do two things: Tell you what the front screen looks like and what on the front screen matches the back end of the database. For example, what's on the front end might be named "shoe," but on the back end you might be looking at product ID "QB1234567." Unless you have someone who can translate what users are seeing up front into what the database is storing at the back, you'll have to go through trial and error to figure it out.

Many times, systems are not fully documented in companies because they have been modified over time or even custom-built. So, in acquiring data from a system, you don't want to make the same mistake that has been made in the past. The best documentation for data acquisition and the best documentation to make your actionable intelligence effort repeatable is a data dictionary. The data dictionary includes the list of elements that you want to have in order to answer a strategic question in plain business terms, as well as a definition of what it's supposed to mean.

After you have spoken with the computer person who explained the logic of how the field is filled in, you can judge how close that comes to the definition you expected. Then you can identify the specific fields and the system or systems that the data comes from. Now you have your data dictionary, and it's repeatable. You know where your data comes from, it is relevant to the question you want to answer, and you know what it means.

The challenge to data acquisition is that you may not be allowed to acquire the data because people have built up silos to protect. People have built jobs—careers—protecting the data, massaging it so it looks just right. So now you come in and say, "Hey—I want your sales data!" It is not likely, even when you are in the same company, that sales data will be shared with you by a different business unit even if it is in a different region. Clearly data acquisition has a human side to it: Will the owner share the data with you? That's why it is important that data acquisition is aligned with the strategic question. If a senior executive has asked you to answer her question, you can go back to that executive and say: "I'm being blocked from getting the data that we agreed was necessary to answer your question." Now the executive can go to the data blocker and say: "Give up your data!" And you have broken down one silo.

It is important that you don't start on the technical side when collecting all the data because then you have no senior-level support. Thus, you will miss the bargaining power to break down silos and gain control of other people's data. Always circle back to the senior-level support throughout this data acquisition process.

This is where the data dictionary will be important. It will tell you who owns the data, who gave you access to the data, how frequently you can get the data, and how you can pull the data in.

The data dictionary is also important because it provides a path for consistency. If someone leaves the acquisition team, for example, the person's replacement can use the dictionary to figure out how to appropriately treat the data.

Timing is also important: Let us say I have up-to-date sales data, but my pricing is not up-to-date. Now I have a problem. If I match up the two, my price and quantity would not line up.

In a global company, it is not unusual to have multiple systems performing planning, warehouse management, data storage, and so on. Figure 3.1 depicts three main challenges you may encounter in mapping data: (1) non-global databases, (2) inconsistent naming conventions, and, worst of all, (3) inconsistent data types.

Start with a simple and clear data dictionary. The example shown in Figure 3.2 is from a data dictionary for a central data repository. Data is organized by CD Table (a table that is in the central repository); CD Field (the name of the field in the table in the central repository); Field Name (the source field name); Table/Source (the table of the source data); Definition (the description of item or object); and Source (the front-end source from which the business data can be seen).

The work of developing the data dictionary must be done by people who are intimate with the business—it simply cannot be outsourced.

When creating a data dictionary, focus on the business description first; the heavy details of data types, field sizes, and technical details will be filled in later. It's important that companies accept the fact that there will be differences in business descriptions and even more important that

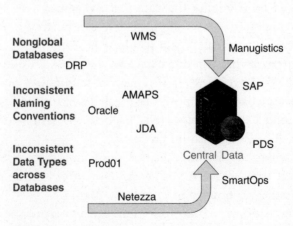

Figure 3.1   Challenges to Map Data

Table(s) to be Updated

Business Need: Access to Shipment information by each supply chain location

Translation Needed?: Yes, convert data from SAP into the Central Database table structure. Only pull in incremental updates

Table Name: tblSCM_MARKET_LAST_SHIP_DATE

CD TABLE	CD FIELD	FIELD NAME	TABLE/SOURCE	DEFINITION	SOURCE
tblSCM_MARKET_LAST_SHIP_DATE	ITEM_ID_6	Base Product Code	tblISAP_SCP_SCM_ZTCGT_EOPL_DATA	The 6 digits represent the brand, item type, and geography of the item	PDS
tblISCM_MARKET_LAST_SHIP_DATE	ITEM_ID_10	Global Product1	tblISAP_SCP_SCM_ZTCGT_EOPL_DATA	The 10 digits represent the entire item code from the Product Defintion System	PDS
tblISCM_MARKET_LAST_SHIP_DATE	LOCATION_ID	Location	tblISAP_SCP_SCM_ZTCGT_EOPL_DATA		
tblISCM_MARKET_LAST_SHIP_DATE	CREATE_DATE	Created on	tblISAP_SCP_SCM_ZTCGT_EOPL_DATA		
tblISCM_MARKET_LAST_SHIP_DATE	CHANGE_DATE	Chngd on	tblISAP_SCP_SCM_ZTCGT_EOPL_DATA		
tblISCM_MARKET_LAST_SHIP_DATE	CHANGED_BY	Changed by	tblISAP_SCP_SCM_ZTCGT_EOPL_DATA		
tblISCM_MARKET_LAST_SHIP_DATE	PLANT_SPECIFIC_ITE	Plant Specific Mater	tblISAP_SCP_SCM_ZTCGT_EOPL_DATA		
tblISCM_MARKET_LAST_SHIP_DATE	DIST_CHAIN_SPECIFI	DC Material Status	tblISAP_SCP_SCM_ZTCGT_EOPL_DATA		
tblISCM_MARKET_LAST_SHIP_DATE	END_SHIP_DATE	End Ship Date	tblISAP_SCP_SCM_ZTCGT_EOPL_DATA		
tblISCM_MARKET_LAST_SHIP_DATE	DATA_FIRMED	ZTCGT_EOPL_DATA-Fil	tblISAP_SCP_SCM_ZTCGT_EOPL_DATA		
tblISCM_MARKET_LAST_SHIP_DATE	TOTAL_REPLENISH_L	Total RL time	tblISAP_SCP_SCM_ZTCGT_EOPL_DATA		
tblISCM_MARKET_LAST_SHIP_DATE	UNIT_MAX_STORAG	Time Unit1	tblISAP_SCP_SCM_ZTCGT_EOPL_DATA		
tblISCM_MARKET_LAST_SHIP_DATE	not needed in CD	Time Unit2	tblISAP_SCP_SCM_ZTCGT_EOPL_DATA		
tblISCM_MARKET_LAST_SHIP_DATE	PHASE_OUT_FLAG	Phase Out Flag	tblISAP_SCP_SCM_ZTCGT_EOPL_DATA		
tblISCM_MARKET_LAST_SHIP_DATE	not needed in CD	Global Product2	tblISAP_SCP_SCM_ZTCGT_EOPL_DATA		
tblISCM_MARKET_LAST_SHIP_DATE	DIRECTION OF INTER	Direction of Interchan	tblISAP_SCP_SCM_ZTCGT_EOPL_DATA		
tblISCM_MARKET_LAST_SHIP_DATE	USE_UP_STRATEGY	Use-up Strategy	tblISAP_SCP_SCM_ZTCGT_EOPL_DATA		
tblISCM_MARKET_LAST_SHIP_DATE	USE_UP_DATE	Use-up Date	tblISAP_SCP_SCM_ZTCGT_EOPL_DATA		
tblISCM_MARKET_LAST_SHIP_DATE	CURRENT_STATUS	Current Status	tblISAP_SCP_SCM_ZTCGT_EOPL_DATA		
tblISCM_MARKET_LAST_SHIP_DATE	GENERATE_PI_RECO	Generate PI Records	tblISAP_SCP_SCM_ZTCGT_EOPL_DATA		
tblISCM_MARKET_LAST_SHIP_DATE	INTERCHANGEABILIT	Group	tblISAP_SCP_SCM_ZTCGT_EOPL_DATA		
tblISCM_MARKET_LAST_SHIP_DATE	GROUP_ITEM_NUMI	Group Item Number	tblISAP_SCP_SCM_ZTCGT_EOPL_DATA		

Figure 3.2 Data Dictionary

business and IT teams work together—and across geographies—to create a common business language to eliminate those differences.

The benefit of the data dictionary is that when you go to write your next intelligence tool, you already know the scope of the data that you have, you're clear on the definitions, and there's an understanding of any discrepancies.

Step 3: Determine the Data Owners, Validate the Data with Them, and Create a Data Dashboard for Those Owners

Now you have determined what data you need, collected the data sets, and documented their most important characteristics in a data dictionary. So what's left? You have the data, but you still don't know whether it's the right data, whether it's correct and complete. And that's something you cannot do all by yourself.

People do not trust data, they trust other people and their opinion of the data. So when the data owners, the people who input the data and/or use it, raise their hands and

The data principle: "People don't trust data, people trust other people."

say, "This data is good; I trust it," that will make it more likely for other people in the organization to believe it. It also means that it's clear. It's not just that they trust it from the point that $1 + 1 = 2$. It is also clear how the data has to be used, and the definition of the data is clear.

However, this does not necessarily mean all your data can be universally validated because not every business unit has the same definitions for its data. For example, Brazil's data may be different from Poland's, but both are right—they just use different rules to measure or input similar information.

If you go to the team in Brazil and ask, "Do these numbers look right to you?"

Brazil might say, "Yes, this matches our source system; we've been using that data to manage our business."

Still, you would double check with Poland and ask, "Do you trust this data? If so, why?"

So now, both Brazil and Poland have validated their data. Now they can trust that data to be true.

But there is another reason to make sure both have raised their hands and said the data is good: Now they're on the hook for the quality of their data, not you.

If you pull in data from different areas and then publish a report, your reputation is at risk. It's important to get all relevant parties to sign off on their data. Now, you're no longer solely on the hook for the data quality.

Placing the data into a centralized spot, understanding it, and making sure it is fit for use is the most important and challenging aspect of the intelligence-gathering project. It also leaves you with important questions: If you succeed, will your effort be sustained? And will your people trust the data, or will you lose control soon, and will data quality decay again?

The data acquisition team needs several tools to be successful in maintaining trust in the data.

- A view of when the data was last updated.
- A list of the tables and the stability of the sources (i.e., was the server up? Were batch jobs completed on time?)
- A review of the changes in data—significant spikes or drops should be at least investigated with the users and IT.

Figure 3.3 is an example of very basic data status, which is easy to start with. Start slow, then move to more advanced analysis.

Figure 3.4 is another view of data health where you can visualize the record counts.

Again, these are simple views, developed quickly to guard against surprise data issues.

Invest a bit of time in protecting the reputation of the intelligence program. But do not make a whole project out of it with fancy tools and deep algorithms until you've received monetized results from the intelligence program.

Step 4: Implement Changes in People, Processes, and Systems to Improve Data Quality

The first three steps constitute important groundwork to make your data acquisition sustainable. However, the last step is about changing people, processes and technology (P, P, and T).

On the people side, you already got the data owners to say they own the data, they're responsible for it, and they have checked it for accuracy.

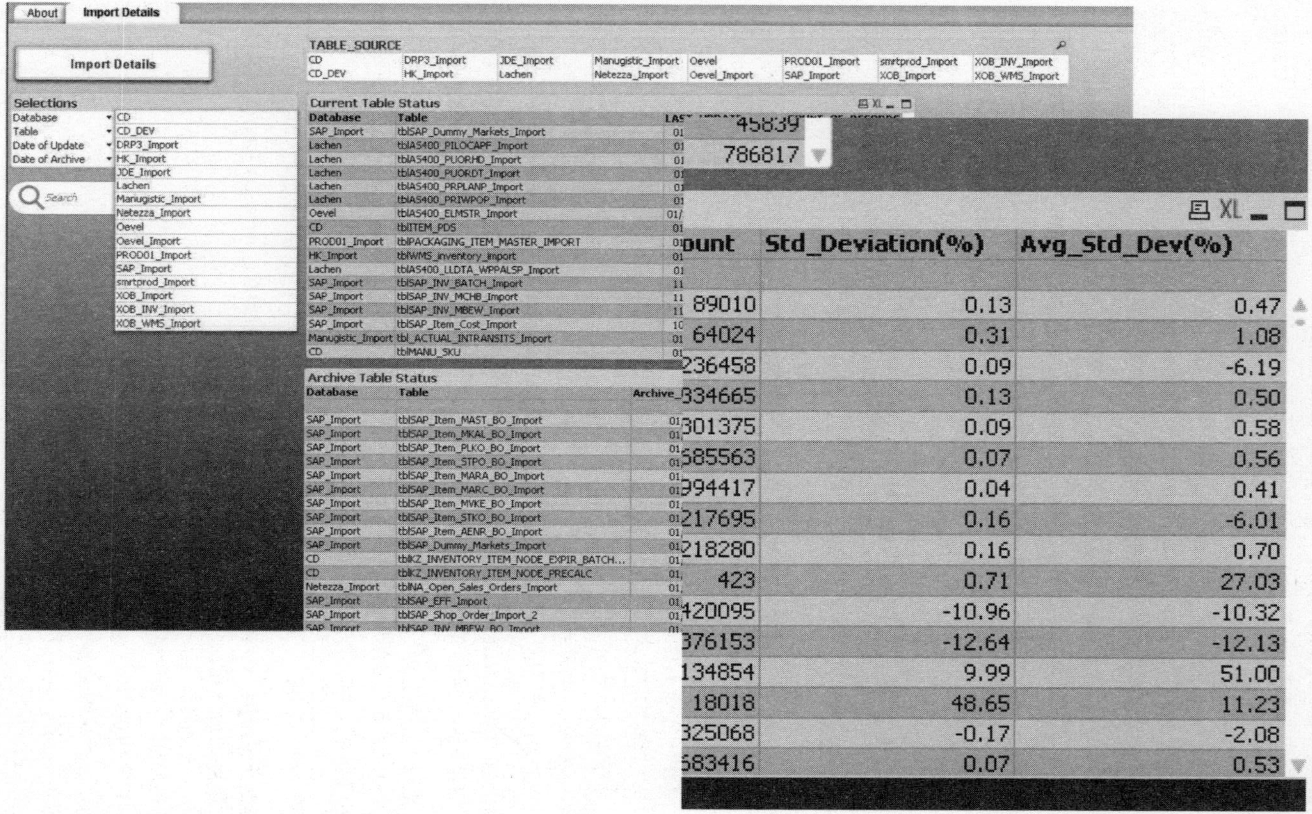

Figure 3.3 Data Acquisition Dashboard

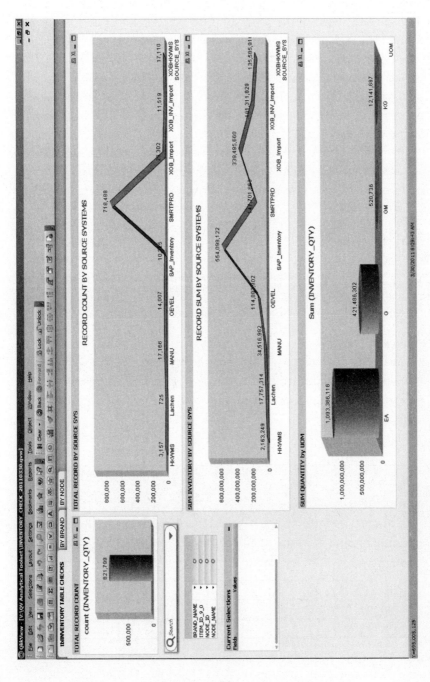

Figure 3.4 Data Acquisition Record Count Dashboard

Now you need to start with the process of measuring all of that information, because what's accurate today can be inaccurate tomorrow and vice versa. Most of the time you find there's a lot of inaccurate data today, and there's an opportunity to make it more accurate tomorrow, because what gets measured improves.

A company might say: "All my sales information is right." Maybe. But haven't you seen or been involved in cases where you wanted to have the finance people close the books for a month but they couldn't because one party lagged in its report?

Companies can't make good decisions using old data, which puts responsibility for data quality squarely on the data owner's shoulders. Indeed, data owners have two responsibilities when it comes to data quality: accuracy and timeliness.

The Data Dashboard   It can be useful to record intelligence in a data dashboard. This dashboard will show the current data situation to yourself and all stakeholders. Figure 3.5 shows a sample data quality dashboard for supply chain.

Some sample key performance indicators explained:

Process Strength
- Green: Standard methodology, complexity mapped, and well-defined
- Yellow: Some standardization, most complexities understood
- Red: Multiple processes to achieve similar goals, complexity not mapped

Data Dashboard				
Business Stage: Supply Chain	Process Stability/ Depth	Input Capability	Review/ Validate Capacity	Recent Problems
Plan				
Source				
Make				
Deliver				

Figure 3.5   Sample Data Quality Dashboard

Input Capability
- Green: Easy, logical to input with bumper rails to avoid errors, right role as owner
- Yellow: Some automation to prevent errors, some propagation/copying
- Red: IRS-like tax form complexity, errors only caught during audit, and painful/costly

Review/Validate Capability
- Green: Validation available to check inputs prior to use by system
- Yellow: Some review reports are available
- Red: Review only possible by re-inputting code, no validation

By the end of the assessment, the chart may mostly be red if there has never been a formal data management team nor supporting key performance indicators to monitor the overall situation. Senior management will become more supportive when they see the easy-to-read chart showing how dire the situation is.

As you start publishing the scorecard, actions will be taken, people trained, and the scorecard will begin to turn from red, to yellow, and to green.

I have reviewed this type of dashboard system with several companies now, and the results are always stunningly . . . red. Whether in New York or Singapore or Japan or Shanghai, the starting dashboards of organizations ranging from banks to universities to manufacturers look mighty scarlet. What color would your organization be today?

The Byproduct: Master Data Management

While building the data foundation to answer your first questions, slowly you realize the process will get easier for you over time. Call it economies of scale. Not every question requires completely new data fields. If you gathered the demand for question 1, you can use that same bit of data for question 2 (provided you need the same data). You documented it already; you validated it. Now the exercise becomes copy-paste. Of course, both questions require you to keep the data up-to-date; answering two questions even gives that data set more priority to be timely and accurate. Ideally, all data sets you use are timely and accurate all the time, but that is a utopia.

The interesting thing is you will slowly create common data sets for the company, shaping and logging the way data fields are named and how they are filled in. You can create, as a byproduct of actionable intelligence, "master data."

Master data is "reference data about an organization's core business entities. These entities include people (customers, vendors, employees), things (assets, products, ledgers), and places (countries, cities, locations).[1]

Take for example data on a sales transaction:

William Smith sold to Teahouse Co. 10 bags of tea leaves for 65 on Jan. 1, 2003.

Now, the separate master data elements used in this transaction are the salesperson (William Smith), the customer (Teahouse Co.), and the product (tea leaves). Each of these elements was listed in master data, to be used and reused time and time again.

So, as a byproduct, what good is master data to you and me? I'll make a clear distinction between byproduct and waste, because, as opposed to waste, having master data and taking it seriously has some major benefits:

- **More accurate and trusted data.** If everyone uses the same master data, errors will be spotted more quickly. Graduating from the tactic of a data dictionary to implementing a full master data strategy provides a fast, stable foundation for future intelligence work.
- **Data consistency.** Master-data management at the enterprise level ensures there will be only one definition for each business term. This does not automatically mean one source of truth or one source of data that renders all other sources obsolete. Businesses need one set of definitions for their business terms, but they can have multiple sources of data.

By applying master-data management as a technique to structure your actionable intelligence efforts, you can achieve more ease of use and fewer errors in the business. You will basically (re)create the data infrastructure of the company, shaping its very existence. All that, just by delivering actionable intelligence. Remember: start with the basics! Master-data management will naturally follow.

Data Management Issues in the Spotlight

Lacking the ability to check on data automatically, companies have become big data checking teams. According to an Oracle survey of its customers across six different industries, "less than 15 percent of organizations surveyed understand the sources and quality of their master data and have a roadmap to address missing data domains."[2]

In addition, it is unlikely there is a process to improve the situation nor is there a scorecard to monitor and evaluate the upstream data entry quality because it's hard to implement and costs money.

So what are some of the best practices to follow initially?

- Establish a senior management meeting to review the data quality of your most strategic questions. Remember, this doesn't mean addressing all the data—focus, focus, focus on the critical elements.
- When the quality isn't up to expectations, know who the data owners are and have them fix it ASAP. There can often be multiple owners because products and services are enriched throughout their lifetimes.
- Engage the business units and business owners to designate problem solvers who are regularly sharing best practices and acting as a first line of defense support with the users who are actually entering information at their desks, in the field, in the warehouse, and so forth.

What should be on a senior management scorecard?
Go back to the strategic question!
Ours were:

- How can we reduce inventory?
- How can we improve service?

A root concern of these questions for master data was, "Are we enriching our master data within the time frame needed to purchase, manufacture, and ship our new products?" So the list of KPIs in Table 3.1 monitored the product data status throughout its life.

Look at a key point—the very first KPI is monetized! How many dollars are impacted by incomplete bills of material? This number woke senior management up right at the beginning of our data review meeting.

Organizationally, you should nominate a single person to be responsible for each step in your business process.

Table 3.1   Example of Key Performance Indicators for Master Data

KPI Name	Detailed Definition	Business Owner
Forecast $'s for incomplete bills of materials	12-month dollarized forecast for finished goods where the BOM is incomplete within eight weeks of shipping date.	Packaging Operations, Industrial Engineering, Planning
# of products with incomplete coding within eight weeks of shipping	The number of finished goods where the BOM is incomplete within eight weeks of plant ship date.	Packaging Operations, Industrial Engineering, Planning
Cycle time to complete product coding	Time from code creation to code complete.	Lead Data Stewards and Plant Local Stewards
# of codes completed per month	The number of codes (finished goods, work in progress, raw materials) completed.	Lead Data Stewards and Plant Local Stewards
Number of codes costed by finance per month	The number of codes that are successfully costed for the given month.	Cost Accounting
% of codes costed	Tracks the % total codes eligible for costing.	Cost Accounting

If the business was a hotel like my favorite, the Grand Hyatt in Singapore, the manager would have a data steward for:

- Marketing and pricing
- Facilities and rooms
- Guest check in/out
- Payment and collections

Or for manufacturing you might have a data steward for:

- Concept and R&D
- Planning
- Make
- Sourcing
- Delivering
- Returns/corporate sales

Senior management is accountable for data quality. In most countries senior managers sign the auditor statements attesting to the accuracy of their books and records. The execution of data quality should be managed and reviewed at least monthly with the above concepts.

The Data Supply Chain

As you pull information together following these four steps, you'll begin to see how data flows in your company. Donald Farmer calls it the "information supply chain."

As shown in Figure 3.6, you can follow your critical data elements through and see their data quality in each stage to ensure the right intelligence delivers the right decisions.

Mapping the data supply chain provides a solid foundation for an actionable intelligence project. It answers the key questions of where is the data, how often is it refreshed, what can we do to trust it, and what's its intrinsic value.

Build the House

Data is an important asset, and your project will be built completely on the data you choose to use. So it is your responsibility to ensure that you have all the data, that the data is timely and accurate, and that your data acquisition is well-documented so you can do it again. You have the power to guide the project to victory, but that power lies not solely in the visualization. The process starts at the foundation.

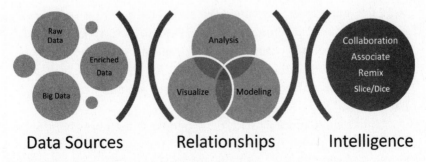

Figure 3.6   Information Supply Chain

When you have the strategic business question and you have the data to answer the question, what's left? The answer, of course! And in order to get to that step, you need to visualize the data with a tool. Then you can apply business discovery to delve through the data with ease and simplicity. So follow the right approach to find the answers to your question!

BAD DATA QUALITY (NOT TIMELY, INACCURATE) IMPACTS LIVES

At the hospital, my mother's condition gradually improved. A few weeks after she first arrived, we prepared to transfer her to a long-term care facility on Long Island, New York. My father and I visited the facility and others on Long Island to find the best place for her to rest, heal, and recover. We visited one particular facility, the Orzac Center for Extended Care & Rehabilitation, several times to make sure they had the right capabilities to support her. Great references, friendly staff—it all looked okay, and it was much closer to home than many other places, so visiting her would be easier.

We received detailed instructions upon checking her out from Columbia University Presbyterian Hospital. The Columbia staff was very courteous, and I felt hope as the ambulance took her to the new facility. My father rode in the ambulance with her, and I followed by car.

It was a Friday afternoon, and driving from New York City to Long Island can take about two to three hours. I arrived much later than my father and mother. By the time I arrived, they were well settled in, pictures placed on the windowsill, Bible on the table.

I felt something was amiss. By 7 P.M., my mother—who was on a ventilator at the time—was supposed to have received food, water, and medication. But it was past 9, and she wasn't being taken care of. The staff at the care facility told me they didn't have the doctor's orders so they couldn't administer anything to her. The hand-off had failed.

Unlike the Columbia staff, these people didn't know anything about my mom—for the next four hours! It was well past midnight by the time she was fed and hydrated. The worst was yet to come.

When they finally took action, they gave her too much food and too much water, too fast. By morning, she was in dire straights again.

Lack of quality data may have been part of my mother's traumatic failure when she arrived at the extended care facility. They were challenged by customer data quality in two ways:

1. The staff may not have had the doctor's orders to feed, hydrate and, medicate her appropriately.
2. Apparently, when the orders were provided, she was given the wrong amount.

My mother ended up in the emergency room, and then the hospital, for the next three days, until we transferred her back to Columbia. It was a safe ground.

Summary and Considerations

Point to Ponder:

- A data dictionary forms the foundation for any actionable intelligence exercise.
- Lives are at stake at health care providers when they don't use their data properly.

Quote to Remember: "People don't trust data. People trust other people and their opinion of the data." —Donald Farmer

Question to Consider: Is there an effective data management scorecard with identified owners measuring data timeliness and accuracy?

Challenge: If you don't have a data quality dashboard, do you know the data is right and your decisions are? There's one way out, which is to say: "We're making the best decision we can with the data we have."

Notes

1. Colin White, "Using Master Data in Business Intelligence," BI Research, March 2007, http://fm.sap.com/pdf/mar09/Using%20Master%20Data%20in%20Business%20Intelligence.pdf.
2. Trevor Naidoo, "Five Key Strategies in Master Data Management," *Profit* (December 2010).

Chapter 4

Visualization

Key Points and Questions

- With the foundation of strategic questions and data, what should we be visualizing?
- How should we be visualizing it?
- Is there a methodology that works?
- How can we continue to move fast, make a difference, and create believers of actionable intelligence?

SOURCE: Lee Min Lau.

Now that you know how to get the data straight and how to visualize that data to arrive at answers, it is time to start building from there. Answering one strategic business question with the aid of great visualizations does not make you a hero instantly. So it is time to move on, increase the effort, and learn from your mistakes to make every new piece of actionable intelligence better, easier, and more visually appealing than the last one.

That is the importance of visualization. You can have important data all cleaned up, full, and complete. If nobody sees it, it has as much added value as an empty bag.

If the data is accurate and timely, as we saw in Chapter 3, then you can unlock its dormant value by making it accessible. Do this by—you guessed it—visualizing the data. Now, the definition of cutting-edge visualization changes every year. What is hip and modern today looks hopelessly outdated tomorrow. That's the reason you will not find images of visualizations in this chapter. Instead, you will find examples of how visualizations develop. And more important, you will learn what elements are in all good visualizations.

Visualizations need to answer "Where we are today?" "Are we happy or sad?" and "How do we win?"

Complete Circle

After putting in place a solid data foundation and starting up our first project at Eséee Lauder, we started to deliver rapid and iterative actionable intelligence. We used a methodology I termed the Project Vision SWAT Iteration Framework (see Figure 4.1).

This fast-paced methodology delivers quick results by asking and answering:

- What's the strategic business question and iterative scope? (Chapter 2)
- Which data is relevant to answer the question? (Chapter 3)
- How should the answer be visualized? (Chapter 4)
- How will the answer be used? What actions taken? What benefits achieved? (Chapter 5)
- Start again and refine the strategic business question.

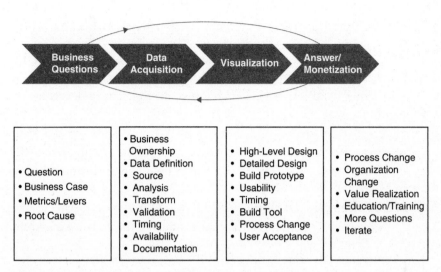

Figure 4.1   Project Vision SWAT Iteration Framework
Copyright © 2012 Keith B. Carter.

Does this work? Yes, says Jack Levis, director of process management at UPS and creator of the amazing ORION project.

Levis manages a team of mathematicians who built the algorithms that help UPS shave millions of miles off delivery routes—ORION, or On-Road Integrated Optimization and Navigation.

When he first brought up the project, his management was skeptical and so were the drivers. He set up competitions between the drivers and the system to refine the model and variables and to acquire more data.

Following an iterative approach and engaging the drivers paid off.

"Starting small shows the project is feasible, optimal, and, more important, implementable. So we created and tested lots of prototypes," Levis told me.[1]

Levis also shared his three key steps to success with me:

Step 1. Prove the concept by delivering real dollars.

Step 2. Build into the process.

Step 3. Provide significant deployment support.

Even with an efficient framework to bring about results, the ORION project was not without its challenges. One of the reasons management was skeptical was that the data seemed impossible to collect.

For example, only the drivers knew external information such as:

- The digital maps in use at the time were not accurate enough. UPS needs to show the exact route to the exact drop-off point, which is sometimes deep into a mall or requires driving several levels into a parking garage.
- The impact of season and weather on a route. Some of the local roads on the map looked crossable in normal GPS maps, but were, in fact, stream crossings that UPS trucks couldn't go through during bad weather.
- School openings and closings that impacted traffic on nearby roads.
- How business customer opening times affected the delivery schedule.

Despite the challenges, the ORION program has been successful. Some of the early benchmarks include:

- 85 million miles saved each year.
- Fuel costs account for less than 20 percent of savings. The main benefit is a reduction in driver time (82 percent of the benefit).
- Theoretically, one mile saved per driver per day in the United States alone saves UPS about $50 million a year.

The ORION program also provides some best practices that any company can apply:

- Manage expectations of management and leave space for improvement.
- Do not do intelligence for intelligence's sake. Think about payback.
- To deliver breakthrough results, be ready to change people's thought process and mindset.

Now that you have established a solid start of your data foundation and an understanding of business discovery, you should have the following support and capabilities in place:

- Some business sponsors of strategic questions
- A data dictionary and standard business language plan
- A talented visualization team
- Business users in the room ready to participate in ideation sessions on where to go

With all the above we had enough ingredients for a successful intelligence project.

Inject speed into the process.
Earl Newsome, former chief technology officer,
Estée Lauder

I was waiting for an elevator, and who walked up but Earl Newsome, a man who knows how to transform organizations fast! But at Estée Lauder, the IT department he was working on changing was struggling.

Newsome shared with me how tough it was to reduce the red tape and get people moving. Then he said a phrase that has stuck with me for years: "We need to inject speed into the process!"

Speed in executing each step is the critical aspect. We established regular ideation sessions 45 minutes in length to agree on visualization or review iterative answers. This framework helped deliver answers in hours and days, satisfying the business' need for speed.

The exciting part of intelligence work is the activity of turning data into easy-to-follow visual representations and then creating stories about how the business is performing today versus opportunities for better performance tomorrow.

Instead of looking at reams of spreadsheets, we delivered the ability to slice and dice intelligence. We brought together streams of data into a single tool to show opportunities for improvement in easy to see red, yellow, and green indicators.

As the users saw the tools during our ideation sessions, they began to develop their own uses and purposes for the intelligence. This enabled us all to run faster toward monetizing the benefits.

The team and I were dedicated to the ideation sessions. While I was on vacation on the beach in Barcelona, we held sessions on one tool. When I was on a cruise ship in the Mediterranean Sea, we held a critical session with the head of supply planning.

Helena May, of the MLH group, held ideation sessions with the demand planning head during the day, at night, and on weekends.

The pace was intense, but the results were worth it.

The users saw where they could use the intelligence on a regular basis. They began to report the results of using the tools to us and regularly asked for improvements. Because we were following the iterative SWAT

Table 4.1   Ideation Session versus SDLC Requirements Gathering

	Ideation Session	Standard Software Development Lifecycle (SDLC) Requirement Gathering Phase
User Involvement	High user involvement High commitment level; involved in all sessions from the start of project	Little user involvement Low commitment level May be absent for certain sessions
Process	Brainstorming and open discussions; fast, proactive, on-the-fly problem solving	Written project brief reports Slow, reactive, waits for approvals from related parties

framework we delivered the changes quickly. The speed of enhancement was a significant departure from standard budgeting methodology and development approach. It was a refreshing change.

Instead of looking at printouts of data from the past, business users received graphical views of past and future performance. Our users were excited, and adoption of the tools increased.

A supply planner in North America said, "This is the first time I can make changes to the plans three months ahead of time, instead of being blamed for shortfalls that happened three months ago."

Here, I'd like to make a distinction between ideation sessions and requirement gatherings. Ideally, ideation sessions are aimed at the users, driven by the users, and demand total involvement every step of the way. Table 4.1 shows the differences between an ideation session and a typical requirement gathering.

So Now, How Can You Do It?

By having the right structure in place, we were able to accelerate from the "beginner" to "localized success" and "enterprise actionable intelligence capabilities" stages of actionable intelligence.

One such structure is the Human Centered Design Toolkit, by International Development Enterprise (IDE). The kit was written to depict the three-theory process that has been commonly used in multinational corporations (see Figure 4.2).

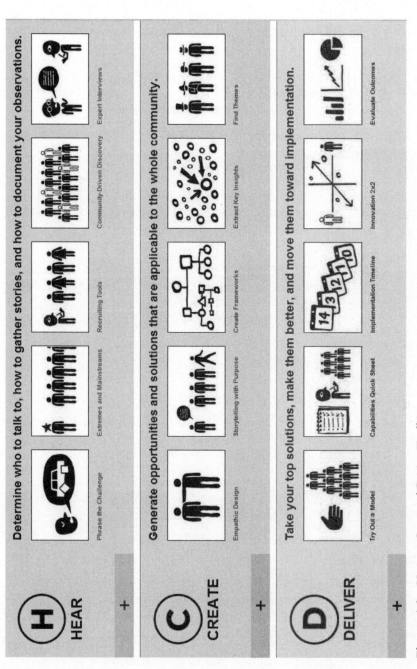

Figure 4.2 Human Centered Design Toolkit

SOURCE: www.hcdconnect.org, www.hcdconnect.org/methods.

75

Hear Phase

1. Determine who to talk to.
    a. Who are the right sponsors, supporters, and who will use the new intelligence to deliver results
2. Determine how to gather stories.
    a. What's the right process in your organization? Can you interview and engage with people?
3. Determine how to document your observations.
    a. How can we work together with team members?

Create Phase

1. Synthesis: Bring information and knowledge together.
    • Gather the appropriate group of individuals (with a range of demographics and backgrounds). Sometimes bringing in some unrelated individuals may provide a new perspective.
    • Share stories.
    • Identify patterns from the existing data.
2. Ideation sessions: Think freely without any constraints, limits, or judgments.
    • Create opportunity areas and move away from analyzing data and toward creating new solutions.
    • Brainstorm new solutions.
3. Prototyping: Make realistic ideas.
    • Structure and improve brainstormed ideas into tangible solutions in a fast and inexpensive manner.
4. Feedback: Improve for the better.
    • Seek critiques and opinions of the team to identify how to improve further.

All these steps should be executed in days, especially prototyping. The resources and permission should be available to execute good ideas as they are created. Enable fast prototyping!

Deliver Phase

In the deliver phase, ideas and solutions created will be implemented to deliver value and results in a sustainable way:

1. Viability check
    • Develop a model that will provide value to the customer, revenue to the organization, and returns to the stakeholders.

2. Capabilities identification
- Source for the required capabilities, manpower. and partners to implement the solution from existing resources or network of contacts.

3. Plan a pipeline of solutions
- Map out how the new solutions move or impact the organization and its strategy for new or existing markets and customers.

4. Conduct mini-tests or pilots

5. Create a learning plan

6. Evaluate and monetize the outcomes

Delivering is important, as is getting the right answer to lots of important strategic business questions. This can be done by anyone because there are a great number of possibilities for the deployment of actionable intelligence.

The Way Ahead

The technology is there, you know the steps to creating actionable intelligence, and your team is ready to step it up. It's now your duty to build actionable intelligence momentum and make the effort reach its tipping point. Grow the project organically until it grows by itself because the organization sees that your project is indispensable to almost every business unit. After reaching that phase, the enterprise actionable intelligence stage mentioned in Chapter 1, the possibilities are endless.

Example of Iterative Visualization to Solve the Question "How Do I Get There Quickly, Safely, Efficiently?": Leveraging Global Positioning System Data

Take this following example: You are driving a car and want to know whether you will arrive safely and on time. It's an old problem with an old solution. A speedometer visualized the data point of your current speed, the gas meter showed whether you still needed to make a stop. Everything else you had to do by yourself. That would be the first iteration of visualizing the available data.

In the 1960s, the U.S. Navy envisioned a new opportunity to move ships effectively and came out with satellite navigational systems. By the time they were made fit for consumers, these systems ran on the Global Positioning System (GPS) and allowed drivers to have a box in their car that calculated where they were, how long the drive was going to take, how far they still had to drive and whether they were keeping to the speed limit.

Iteration two, the navigational system to add on to iteration one, was elegantly designed and visualized all the information it gathered in such a way that the user only needed one glance at the little box to see what needed to be seen.

Even though iteration two doesn't show whether the user will be there on time, the navigational system will come pretty close. Users can answer that question for themselves, and hooking up the schedule to the navigational system could lead to visualizing the answer to that question.

However, there is one word in the strategic question—"Will I make it safely and on time?"—I left out. Currently, no system takes into account safe driving.

So that brings us to iteration three—one we haven't realized yet. To show whether you can drive safely and be on time, we need to layer in traffic conditions on the road, weather conditions, police speed traps, and so on. We also need to know how likely the car is to break down—on major points like tires, brakes, and lights. Some systems still provide this information, but most systems stop before reaching this point. By visualizing this you could give a basic answer as to whether you will arrive safely and on time (and without tickets).

We can go deeper still to iteration four. It is possible to realize systems that monitor whether you have been on a certain stretch of road before, whether your average speed is up on that stretch, and how many accidents have occurred on that same stretch. By monitoring biometrics you could also tell whether you are intoxicated, have a low pulse, feel sleepy, or have an illness that interferes with your ability to drive. Let's call this harder-to-get data really big data.

While you are driving you need a very fast answer. The answer needs to be simple, visual, and nondistracting. You can't afford to be distracted by, for example, your current heart rate, on top of everything else being displayed in your car. When you need the answer, you need it fast. You can't do the whole analysis while driving.

So this leaves us with one question: What would this visualization look like? I'd suggest a big view with clear colors indicating whether you are making it and whether you are safe. If you want to know by how much, you should be shown an estimate of the difference in travel time. If you want to drill down, you should have the option to say to your little black box "tell me the factors delaying me," and the box would list them.

Whether you were at iteration one or iteration four, there were some commonalities in the example.

- You want the answer as quickly as possible. Why would you have a visualization if it only requires more work? The aim of visualizing data is to instantly get a picture of what the organization looks like. The same was true for every iteration in the car. You can get the answer instantly, without having to do anything.

- We want to visualize the relationships as clearly as possible. Ideally, there should be no ambiguity as to what the visualizations mean, how the data must be interpreted, and how the different sets of data link together. While driving, you need to be shown how each of the factors increases or decreases your safety or driving time. That way you know how you can alter your driving or bodily state to be more optimal.

- A visualization brings together data from multiple departments, placing it on one screen in a logical way so that cross functional discussions can be held easily. It creates an overall picture across different information silos. Your heart rate in a car doesn't mean anything by itself, but in combination with various other metrics, your black box can reach a conclusion on how fit you are to drive.

- You need to be able to tell a story: What do these numbers mean? What does the situation mean, or what should I do? Why? How should we go about that? The navigational system gives you the routes, the information. It's up to you to figure out how you determine the journey to arrive on time and safely. The navigational system is not giving you the final step, it's not automatically taking you there.

As soon as machines take over the process of interpreting the answer, making the decisions, and reflecting on those decisions, management can be fired and robots can take over the business. Until then you need to be able interpret the story behind the data, the story behind what the numbers tell you.

Effective Visualizations: Tell a Story to Your Mind

Why are we visualizing information in a particular way? Why do bar charts and pie charts work better than tables? The answer is simple. It's because of how our minds work. We trigger a bigger area in our brains when we look at data ordered in a way that comes naturally to us than we do by looking at raw data. Raw data, lists, and tables require us to think in order to understand the data and piece together the relationships in our minds. Visualizations let you see the relationships visually and instantly. This works because our minds use heuristics to determine what goes together, and data visualizations use those same heuristics to show people what they need to know.

Early in the twentieth century the Gestalt school of psychology, developed by Christian von Ehrenfels and inspired by Hume, von Goethe, and Kant, determined how the mind sees relationships between points and pieces of drawings. This led to mapping some important heuristics that to this day remain valid and the basis of many visualizations.

Table 4.2 provides a short list of the heuristics the mind uses.

These heuristics are interesting and explain why certain visualizations work so well. Though when you keep in mind just the list of commonalities we discussed earlier when creating visualizations, you will almost always automatically adhere to one or more of these heuristics, because your brain knows what makes information easiest for it to understand.

Noticing Visualization Pitfalls

In the end you are still the user of the tools you create to visualize the business. The tools will not make your decisions nor give you the relationships. They are called tools because they give you the means to find relationships and make the decisions.

Table 4.2   Human Heuristics

Proximity	Objects that are close to each other are assumed to belong together.	You probably feel a connection to the nearest city as opposed to some place on the other side of the country.
Similarity	Objects that are perceived as equal are assumed to belong together.	Tigers and lions go together much better than tigers and fish. They are similar.
Enclosure	Objects enclosed by a line or plane are assumed to belong together.	All the things on a desk are assumed to be of one person; all the things not on there are assumed to be of someone else.
Closure	Objects that are not fully finished will be assumed to be finished in the mind.	If you stare into a crescent moon, you will likely see the outlines of a full moon. The mind does this.
Continuation	Objects that disappear partially behind other objects are continued in the mind.	To see this, all you have to do is shove one item in front of another.
Connection	Objects linked together by anything whatsoever are assumed to belong together.	Connection is very easy; you'll associate almost everything that is connected to each other physically as a group.

The Post Hoc Fallacy

One of the biggest pitfalls here is the fact that you still have to find the relationships for yourself. This sounds easy but can lead to what practitioners call the post hoc fallacy. The post hoc fallacy means you see relationships that aren't there, just because the data suggests such relationships. This nasty trap can be avoided by clear and careful thinking when determining relationships suggested by the data. Does the relationship make sense? Is it causal one way or another? Or is there just a correlation? The famous example from statistics is this: On days where people buy more ice cream, more people drown. So people drown because of ice cream? No! People drown because there are a lot of people in the sea on hot days. And on hot days more ice cream is sold. There is a relationship, but no causation between ice cream sales and drowning. So be aware; use your logic.

Earlier I mentioned that statistical forecasts that do not include the right amount of data and influences are good for matching the past but not for predicting the future. Many organizations talk about "forecast accuracy" with decimal points as if to appear very precise. The reason business leaders aren't satisfied is because the forecast is often wrong and there is a cost associated with errors in either poor customer service or increased costs.

This was made very clear in the April 6, 2014, *New York Times* article "Eight (No, Nine!) Problems with Big Data," by Gary Marcus and Ernest Davis.[2]

> [Even] when the results of a big data analysis aren't intentionally gamed, they often turn out to be less robust than they initially seem. Consider Google Flu Trends, once the poster child for big data. In 2009, Google reported—to considerable fanfare—that by analyzing flu-related search queries, it had been able to detect the spread of the flu as accurately and more quickly than the Centers for Disease Control and Prevention. A few years later, though, Google Flu Trends began to falter; for the last two years it has made more bad predictions than good ones.

Visualization should first be used to identify a situation holistically, with a wider field of vision. Too often, scientists attempt to hone in on a correlation right away. This is like looking at the stars through a telescope when there is an elephant in your way. You find very interesting constellations, until you step back and realize it's not the stars you are seeing but an elephant's hide!

The authors of the *New York Times* article also warn about making too many connections.

> If you look 100 times for correlations between two variables, you risk finding, purely by chance, about five bogus correlations that appear statistically significant—even though there is no actual meaningful connection between the variables. Absent careful supervision, the magnitudes of big data can greatly amplify such errors.

Organizations can avoid these problems by maintaining focus on the big picture and the original strategic question.

Summary and Considerations

Points to Ponder: With regular, short bursts of engagement, business owners can feel true ownership about the visualization.
Quote to Remember: "Be aware; use your logic."
Question to Consider: What would your ideal visualization answer?

Notes

1. Keith Carter, "Big Data: A Framework for Action," NUS Business School Think Business (October 2013), http://thinkbusiness.nus.edu/articles/item/156-big-data-a-framework-for-action.
2. www.nytimes.com/2014/04/07/opinion/eight-no-nine-problems-with-big-data.html?_r=0.

Chapter 5

The Initial Answers

Key Points and Questions

- The next step in business intelligence.
- Get the project up to speed.
- Keep measuring the results to win over and satisfy sponsors.

Congratulations. By the time you reach this stage, you should be able to answer your first strategic business questions with a satisfying answer. Was that it? Is it done now?

No! We must measure the results, plus understand the monetary benefits and the soft benefits to justify developing after even more actionable intelligence.

Actionable intelligence can be used in many different ways, both proactively and—sometimes, in the face of disaster—reactively. It is with the latter that a company's actionable intelligence capabilities are truly put to the test.

On March 11, 2011, we arrived at work hearing about a terrible tragedy. Japan had been hit by an earthquake and a tsunami—lives were lost, and nuclear meltdown loomed. Our CEO convened a crisis management council to determine the welfare of our employees in Japan, how we could assist the people of Japan, and what was the impact on our business.

We received a call with a request to provide intelligence about our business including the risk to supply, sales, and so on.

We created an analysis that showed:

- Our current global inventory at manufacturing, distribution, and suppliers
- Production plans that could be impacted by a decline in raw materials sourced from Japan
- Suppliers and customers impacted by the crisis

My team delivered the information to the crisis management team on the same day. A complete assessment of the impact of the crisis on 200-plus supply chain nodes, more than 10,000 SKUs across more than 26 brands and more than 100 countries.

These results helped guide the crisis management team with facts. One senior executive called it "magic!"

He added, "Without the actionable intelligence capabilities of your team, we may never have received this level of detail."

A recent article noted the need for supply chain leaders to implement end-to-end supply chain visibility.[1] This article stressed the need for actionable intelligence. It reinforced something we experienced firsthand when the earthquake hit.

I was very glad to see we had increased our capabilities in the right direction. Instead of simply gathering big data and upsizing old systems, we delivered new, useful capabilities.

Companies and governments should not be collecting big data just for the sake of data. They should be focusing on using data to find answers to the strategic business questions that deliver life-changing results. At Estee Lauder, we were able to control the disruptions caused by the disaster and risks to the company that could have been translated into the loss of hundreds of jobs. The benefits of leveraging big data to find answers should result in continued employment for the company's workers because the company is able to maintain its operations. In addition, there will be better employment opportunities because the type and quality of work the team is doing is smarter and higher.

Attempting to Regularly Capture Benefits, False Starts, and a Rhythm

To build on the success of end-to-end visibility, start gaining broader support for intelligence by showing measurable results from its use.

I tasked my entire team with gathering comments, feedback, and information from various parts of the organization. I put up a thermometer in the office, like the ones you see in front of fund-raising organizations. It was big, and at the top it had a goal of $1 million. I said to the team in one of our meetings, "Everyone needs to bring in the monetized benefits of intelligence."

I expected us all to find savings and even made it part of our goals and objectives.

A week or two went by and nothing . . . I was quickly losing hope.

Then, Kristin Zellner, a bright, sparkly-eyed, energetic woman, started presenting me with quotes and savings from business users. She had taken her own initiative to work with supply chain team members to monetize the use of intelligence. The users who gave us the quotes also benefited. Their names went up in lights! I call these resume builders. Anytime you can show you have delivered money to an organization, other organizations are going to want you to do the same for them.

It benefits the intelligence team because now the monetized results are associated with the project, and you have an ambassador in the business who will share this information with team members.

Finally, I wrapped this effort into a process by which Kristin would update my status report to my boss with the latest quotes and savings. This showed we were delivering results from the beginning.

Make sure you or someone on the team is performing this role of monetizing results.

The Results of Actionable Intelligence Delivered

On the very first week we held training, a supply planner used our intelligence tools to deliver $200,000 in customer service!

Once users know there's a problem, they can drill into the item to see where it's made and where the customers are globally, in an instant.

POLITICS OF CAPTURING QUOTES
AND BENEFITS

Danger comes from all sides. Top IT management, your boss, and other senior business leaders become concerned if too much light is shining on the actionable intelligence team.

While good leaders should support the success of their organization, chalk it up to human nature. Someone will say, "These results don't prove anything" or "People are uncomfortable with your quotes."

Ignore it.

If you are on the intelligence team or leading it, these quotes and savings are your currency to buy continued support from the sponsors. No one can deliver more support in an organization than the team that harnesses big data to help their colleagues make better decisions.

Without our tools, the supply planner would not have easy visibility into whether his product is on track for delivery because his product could be made in locations that were not connected into the central Enterprise Resource Planning (ERP) system. To understand the full picture, he may have needed to look into 14 different systems as well as send e-mail to other departments for additional information.

For this specific instance, Global Days of Supply showed the item was a new launch and made in Belgium. The supply planner and Kristin called the planner in Belgium to ask why the supply orders weren't showing up. The planner said, "Oh! The Manufacturing Resource Planning (MRP) flag is turned off in our planning system. We have all the raw materials, but it would never have been made on the production floor!"

Out of 10,000 products, one wasn't set correctly . . . another data quality management issue, but this time visualized and acted on to improve the outcome.

Kristin asked the supply planner how much this finding was worth in customer service protection. He calculated we would have missed the launch and it would have risked $200,000 in planned sales.

This first event nearly covered the project cost up to this point in one day. That was *really* exciting!

It was the turning point that enabled the business team to go from being reactive to being proactive about protecting the supply chain and turned the discussion from "what happened?" to "we are taking action to make the future even better."

We began to receive several quotes a week about benefits the tools delivered to the company.

Through gathering quotes at Estée Lauder we delivered more than $87 million in the first 10 months—much more than the cost to implement actionable intelligence. In fact, had I predicted that we would achieve this amount of monetized benefits for the business, no one would have believed me. I would not have believed it myself. The best part of this effort was the fact that the user community raised their hands throughout the year to share the benefits they themselves had found.

The Power of Quotes

By collecting all these hard benefits and user quotes, we slowly built a powerful case to convince business sponsors the project was worth its cost. Existing sponsors kept our efforts up and running, while new sponsors joined in as they became convinced of the benefits of actionable intelligence. In the end, success builds more success, more resources, and more capabilities. Never forget that you need success first to rally support, before you can start increasing your efforts.

Possibilities with Actionable Intelligence

At Estée Lauder, we saw how actionable intelligence allowed us to realize millions of dollars in savings in the production and manufacturing aspect of the supply chain. However, the possibilities with actionable intelligence do not end there. Following are examples of how businesses can use actionable intelligence:

Social Media Sentiments

Social media has traditionally been the domain of marketing. Scanning e-mails, tweets, and posts and analyzing the frequency, semantic relationships, writing styles, sentence structure, and relative importance of certain words or phrases from Facebook or Twitter can tell a lot about the writer of the posts. Social media sentiment analysis can help companies to:

- Understand their customers' opinions, why consumers are upset with the brand, and what they will say about it to their friends.
- Identify areas for improvement and innovation.
- Improve their reputation and branding; food and beverage companies should be on top of their various platforms, rating their establishments to attract new customers as well as to retain old ones. Too many potential customers may be impacted by reviews made by users in forums.
- Enhance demand by visualizing where social media is indicating the customer is and where the project is, and identify where consumers in need of their product are and get the customer service to work with them to meet their specific needs.
- Utilize the power of social media to help identify customers at various stages of life. This will allow them to offer the appropriate service or product, for instance, help banks identify people in the market for life insurance, joint saving accounts, saving plans for a house, or mortgages. Studying social media allows a company to be highly responsive to specific customer needs.

. . . but there's more. By connecting social media to the supply chain we can deliver faster insights to determine:

- Use of the products and services by consumers
- Availability of the product/services at the location and time customers want to buy
- Perception of quality in the customers' view.

Companies should ensure this information quickly flows to the operations areas to respond as needed. Make sure to establish a solid information supply of social media data by establishing a play book to clearly define the actions to be taken when customers share their concerns on social media. Plan the steps that marketing, customer service, and supply chain will take.

Supply chain normally has responsibility for quality assurance. Keep in mind social media can be an extension of the QA department to rapidly test and receive customer insights.

Execution Excellence

More often than not, there are events that lie beyond an organization's control and affect its ability to execute 100 percent perfectly. However, by collecting information about the difference between the actual versus the planned execution method, companies can get one step closer to achieving execution excellence.

- Identify bottlenecks, causes of error, and challenges. Determine the root cause for low performance and utilization of resources. Is there a section along the production line that is slowing down production or creating a large number of defective products? Understand the challenges faced by the employees working in that section and take actions to either remove the bottleneck or increase the capacity at the bottleneck.
- Optimize the use of resources. Can resources be further utilized to improve productivity? Is there an over allocation of manpower in one department that has caused the marginal efficiency of employees to be falling? How can employees be reassigned to a different department to improve overall efficiency?
- Improve and ensure quality standards. Manufacturing products of the right quality will not only result in savings of time, money, and effort needed to correct defects, but it will also help to maintain customer loyalty and trust in the brand.

Prediction of Future Performance

For public companies, there is a routine of predicting company performance for financial investors and analysts. When targets are not met, investors and analysts will suffer, too. With intelligence on near-real-time information about company operations, companies will be able to:

- Identify emerging trends. Use competitive intelligence to see where competitors are falling down either in supply chain (not enough

products) or in branding. Analyze these areas and seize opportunities where the organization can enter and serve that group of consumers.
- Make more accurate predictions.
- Take action to counter threats or seize opportunities.

Cost Management

Costs are the bottom line of the company and the higher the line, the smaller the profits gained from the top line of sales. With intelligence, companies can take actions to achieve the optimal solution to the following questions:

- Based on our best demand and supply plans, what is the cost of acquiring each customer and the revenue to be earned from them in the next 12 to 18 months?
- What could cause the costs to increase and what can we do to lower the cost in the future?
- Where is the lowest cost to serve to our future customers based on market expansion plans and demand?
- What is the range of profit targets we may achieve if we serve this channel at this volume of sales and with this margin?
- Based on all the above, what could our margins be in the next quarter, half-year, year, and what target can we safely set?
- These questions need to be answered at a corporate, regional, and local level with visibility through the entire enterprise to optimize the results. Set the expectation of daily visibility to risks and easy access to information to seize opportunities.

Mergers and Acquisitions

The time that companies have to offer or accept an acquisition or merger varies greatly. Having the right information at hand with the right algorithms to calculate the risk and return on investment helps provide an objective review of the target company. Of course it can be difficult to acquire the data necessary, but the value of gathering the data is very high:

- You will get an early start on integrating the companies, which translates into faster return on investment via synergy and shared services.

- Seeing the data enables a realistic assessment on whether the rolled-up numbers are accurate.
- Having a team and process in place sets the table for future acquisitions to go well.

Key questions to ask include:

- Identify the potential savings or losses. Would the cost of acquisition threaten the financials of the company? Is the value of the company likely to experience exponential growth in the near future? Tony Hsieh of Zappos rejected an acquisition offer of $2 million for his first company, LinkExchange, only to be acquired by Microsoft a year later for $265 million.
- Leverage customer, workforce, or operational synergies. Will the merger bring about economies of scale from the combined volume of activities and products from the two companies? Will this free up more manpower to perform higher value-adding tasks? Will the reputation, image, and branding of one company complement or compete against the other?
- Seize the right opportunity, What are the emerging trends that might be blind spots for our competitors. Are they falling down either in supply chain (not enough products) or in branding. Are there areas where your organization can enter and serve that group of consumers that doesn't yet feel satisfied?

Manufacturing, Operations, and Quality

As one of the areas in the company with the longest usage of intelligence, operations and manufacturing are well-known for the Total Quality Management and Six Sigma methodologies. With actionable intelligence, operations can go beyond just measuring yield or adopting a reactive approach:

- Determine capital investment. Simulate scenarios to balance the pros and cons of investing in new equipment. Will the purchase of equipment with a higher production capacity lower the unit cost with fewer production runs or will it overproduce items that will result in wastage?
- Alert users about major potential quality or system failure issues early and proactively. In 2013, the Chief Information Officer (CIO)

of Komatsu K.K. Kosuke Yamane and I met, and he told me a piece of the latest technology being put in their big equipment is a complete monitoring system that communicates the health, location, and status of the equipment. This data can be used to proactively maintain the equipment for customers thereby reducing lost work time and protecting customer goodwill.

- Proactively receiving almost-real-time information will enable the organization to strategize resource reallocation countermeasures instead of using a reactive fire-fighting approach.
- Manage the sales order book to optimize margins by sharing the timing of new launches; orders and quotes can be timed to protect margin opportunities.

Testing and Getting the Right Formula

Gut feeling alone is not enough anymore because business has become very global and very complex. Actionable intelligence and hard facts augment gut feeling, providing leaders with new planning capabilities. We can use actionable intelligence to understand whether we are doing things the right way and reaching out to customers in the most effective way. Online platforms and websites use intelligence to their advantage. They:

- Utilize heat maps to identify which areas of a page receive the most attention, activity, and approval. How long are consumers spending on the website and what is the hit rate like? Why are they leaving so quickly? Where are visitors hovering around on the website? Where did they stop?
- Maximize the consumer experience by making the appropriate changes.
- Experiment and pilot-test all aspects of the websites before the full, official launch. Gather consumer intelligence and identify the best way to launch with a bang.

Health Care and Healthier Living

The discomfort when we get sick is not just the feeling of illness we contend with. This discomfort is coupled with the financial concern about the medical bills associated with diagnosis and treatment. Intelligence can enable professionals in the health care and insurance sectors to provide better services to patients and their families:

- Make predictions about the likelihood of health insurance buyers getting more severe diseases. Are clients paying the right premiums for the plans? Is the insurance company bearing too much risk? If the client has a family background of certain diseases, should they be serviced with a better plan?
- Conduct medium-term demand planning to prepare for the influx of hospital cases. Is there sufficient information available to help the hospital make the necessary preparations to provide the required care, attention, and treatment to the largest number of patients in the fastest, most efficient manner?
- Enable caregivers to make better diagnoses using an intelligent learning system that brings together clinical trial results with doctor observations, and social media feedback from consumers. Leveraging this big data helps care providers make the right decisions for patients.

Other questions include:

- How can doctors reduce the pressure in the decision-making process for the caregivers?
- Can the availability of medical records and better accuracy in the prognosis help them to make the right decision and justify that decision to the rest of the family?

Attracting and Retaining Customers

In marketing, there are several ways to reach out to the target group and segment. However, with so many mediums out there, which is the right one to invest in to bring in customers? Intelligence can provide the appropriate justification that will enable marketers to allocate their budgets to the right efforts to reach out to the right customer:

- Identify the appropriate mix of marketing mediums to reach out to the right group of people. If the target audience is a group of retired elderly, should the medium be social media platforms or should it be television advertisements?

- Reward loyal customers with customized services and discounts. According to Tony Hsieh CEO of Zappos the company rewards its customers by upgrading their purchases from the standard delivery to an overnight delivery. This incentivizes customers to make repeat visits and become loyal advocates of the brand.
- Avoid bad customers while attracting the stars. Who should be attended to: the guy in the turtleneck sweater and jeans who looks like Steve Jobs or the man in the suit? Should customers be profiled based only on their looks, or is there more information that can be used?

On a global level, the marketing team needs to provide sales and supply chain with market share estimates and the impact on demand forecasts, inventory, and supply. Combining price optimization with consumer migration patterns and in-depth looks at point-of-sale activity of a brand leader can provide better fact-based estimates.

Business Capabilities for Insurers

Insurers should be actively pursuing intelligence initiatives in three key areas: customer-centric, risk-centric, and finance-centric activities. Figure 5.1 identifies a number of important areas where intelligence is already being applied by leading insurers. Many of these areas have significant potential to create an even larger business impact through the use of high-performance intelligence.

In meeting with insurance companies in the United States and Japan, it is clear that while they are highly analytical about risk, most lack depth of customer knowledge. Actionable intelligence will enable insurers to make customer decisions in real time, even as interactions are in process.

Risk Intel	Customer Intel	Finance Intel
☐ Underwriting	☐ Identification	☐ Modeling
☐ Pricing	☐ Cross-Sell	☐ Portfolio Optimization
☐ Fraud	☐ Retention	☐ Liability Coverage
☐ Reserves		

Figure 5.1   Actionable Intelligence Opportunities: Insurance

Insurers can identify potential customers by linking their extensive internal information with external data including social media, political, economic risks, and more.

According to a study by A. T. Kearney,[3] car insurers can help lower insurance rates for good drivers by monitoring their behavior using a system installed in their car called *telematics*. The system provides information about speeding and reaction to driving conditions, which can be analyzed to assess a 20 to 30 percent discount in insurance rates.

The same system can be used to improve driving habits by tracking the length of time the driver was on the road, and a warning can be issued when the driver may be tired or when the brake too hard.

The association of British Insurers calculated the industry has not made an underwriting profit since 1994. Insurance claims and the costs to insure resulted in a £289 loss in 2013 according to their study "UK Insurance Key Facts 2013." [2]

The opportunity telematics and actionable intelligence provide is to bring this back into a profitable range by rewarding good drivers and improving bad drivers. Several new business models can be put in place according to the AT Kearney study:[3]

- Pay As You Drive: A device installed in the vehicle validates the mileage and location allowing for more accurate risk and thus cost.
- Pay How You Drive: An accelerometer provides event data on sharp turns, hard braking, or fast acceleration. This could be particularly helpful for fleets with significantly higher risks of property damage, fatality, loss of business, and reputation. Both the insurer and business could take proactive steps to improve driving behavior. It would also be a great fact-based driving record for future employers.

If the car and insurance industry don't jump on this, we'll be sure to see consumers leveraging a mobile phone app that provides evidence-based driving records to challenge insurance premiums.

Pricing Optimization

The reservation price of each consumer is different. Charging every consumer the same price is not necessarily optimal. Having intelligence into the reservation price of each consumer will enable the organization to identify the right price for the right customers.

- Consider the opportunities for dynamic pricing. In the United States, even within the same state, online retailers provide a different price to a customer using a Windows computer and one using a Mac.
- Identify the appropriate price and value of a product or service. Amazon and other auction websites or retailers that have a bidding system allow consumers to decide the optimum price.
- A consumer from Russia may travel to certain cities via a connecting flight through the United Kingdom on the way to New York, for example. A brand that knows the flight pattern based on data collected from travel agencies, hotels, and social media can look at its product pricing and optimize the price so the consumers react the way the brand wants them to. In Hong Kong and China, for example, brands quickly saw their Hong Kong store sales increase as Chinese consumers began travelling. The knowledge of the huge price differences between Hong Kong and China attracted both individual consumers and smart businesspeople, who bought pallets of product at a time. They would simply cross the border into Guang Zhou and resell at a discount to the consumers in China.

Note that this list is by no means comprehensive! Actionable intelligence is usually not limited by technology. The barrier lies in the creativity of the user. Any piece of data can be turned into intelligence by organizing and visualizing, even your breakfast.

Almost Done?

When your project gets invigorated, that's when you will strike. That's the tipping point, the critical mass that will be reached to do great things. So is there anything left? Why, certainly, yes there is. In dealing with people, processes, and technology, so far most of what we have done is aimed at technology and its direct implementation. The next chapter deals with changing and adapting to processes in the organization. Chapter 7 will be about the people and making the effort sustainable over the long run.

I've mentioned cases for how actionable intelligence can be used in multiple industries. New cases and opportunities are being written every day. Please take a look at my website www.keithbcarter.com to find out the latest opportunities for your business.

Summary and Considerations

Point to Ponder: Performance metrics drive behavior. Make sure you are driving the right behavior.
Quote to Remember: "Inject speed into the process!"
Question to Consider: What do you need to do to capture and monetize the benefits?

Note

1. Mary C. Holcomb, Serhiy Y. Ponomarov, and Karl B. Manrodt, "The Relationship of Supply Chain Visibility to Firm Performance," *The Best of SCM Research* (2010).
2. Association of British Insurers, "UK Insurance Key Facts" (September 2013).
3. Joe Reifel, Mike Hales, Gang Xu, and Shamik Lala, " Telematics: The Game Changer Reinventing Auto Insurance," AT Kearney (2010).

Chapter 6

Time for Change

Key Points and Questions

- Work with business leaders to embed the fact-based decision making into their processes.
- Establish cross-functional/regional collaboration to properly leverage actionable intelligence.
- Break down the silos, access your own data.
- Is your governance structure giving you the money or asking you the question first?
- How do you persuade sponsors to put money on the table?
- Don't become mired in cost discussions. The visibility will bring many more benefits than cost, both hard measurable benefits and soft ones.
- Portion of your life are online; should you be concerned?
- Data security: How do you guard against spies and breaches?

This statement by Helgerson should give pause to every business leader, every human resources person, and every change agent. The U.S. government on boards incoming presidents long before

CIA PRESIDENT'S DAILY BRIEF: A SOLID EXAMPLE OF CROSSFUNCTIONAL ACTIONABLE INTELLIGENCE

"Since 1952 the Central Intelligence Agency of the U.S. government has provided presidential candidates and presidents-elect with intelligence briefings during their campaigns and transitions. Their briefings have helped presidents be as well informed as possible on international developments from the day they take office."

Source: "Getting to Know the President," John L. Helgerson, retired CIA inspector general.

they take office, providing them with intelligence, which they can turn into action on the first day they take office. This is the gold standard for bringing new staff onboard at any level. The president is trained on the process, method, and purpose of his role as a decision maker before his first day.

The purpose of briefing presidential candidates and presidents-elect is to give them a head start on implementing defense tactics as soon as they assume office.

After taking office, the chief executive receives something called the President's Daily Brief (PDB), prepared by the Central Intelligence Agency (CIA) and tailored to each executive's style and focus. For example, the CIA established a very good relationship with President Reagan and provided him with economic, political, and military opportunities. The end of the Cold War and takedown of the Berlin Wall was helped, in large part, by the CIA's PDBs, which provided insight into how the Soviet Union leaders would respond to economic relationships. Reagan is still credited today with this tremendous success during his presidency.

In contrast, the relationship between President John F. Kennedy and the CIA was strained, according to Helgerson. The information provided to him by the CIA was not as timely or accurate as it needed to be. This contributed to several mis-steps including the Cold War incident called the "Bay of Pigs."

By President Ronald Reagan's time, the CIA had set the bar high, operating a sophisticated and well-oiled intelligence machine. As one of the world's largest intelligence agencies, that's its job.

How often do you brief your leadership and key customers on risks and opportunities? Even if you could do so regularly, would they understand the information and act on it?

To gain the same benefits from intelligence as US policy makers from the CIA you will need to change the way you acquire, validate, and consume intelligence throughout your enterprise. There will no doubt need to be some changes in governance, budgeting, security, sales, and operations planning. By leading change you will do more than just reinforce the core of actionable intelligence; you will integrate the processes of the entire organization with your own.

By now you probably have technology ready; you'll also be surprised at the talent available within your organization when you provide them with data, but these need to be focused toward the goal of answering strategic business questions to be fully effective.

Collaborative Business Planning

The real champions of delivering business results are the people who can successfully instate the process of collaborative business planning. This sounds very simple, but it can be a daunting task. Various business functions are often aligned against each other because they have opposing key performance indicators (KPIs). Take sales and operations for example. The demand for fast delivery of products to the clients by the sales team clashes with the operations team's capacity to deliver balancing speed, cost, and quality. Sudden demand spikes may require the operations team to work overtime resulting in higher costs of production and, thus, conflict with the finance team's expectations of lower costs.

By bringing all departments together in a regular meeting armed with equal access to intelligence, issues, problems, challenges, and bottlenecks can be brought out for discussion. In addition, through the ideation sessions discussed in Chapter 4, all departments can work together to overcome those issues and agree on the targeted sales for the company, how operations and purchasing will support the manufacturing and delivery of the required goods, and what the targeted top and bottom lines for the year will be.

Companies can be more efficient when they go back to where they started from: having all the business teams in the same room to optimize business performance.

Let us go back to that original situation all companies begin in. When a company first started, the founder has the passion and the strategy. The sales team is in the same room as operations, and manufacturing or services is also nearby. As the company expands, sales moves out to a fancy office somewhere else; operations stays with the plant. Sometimes different sales and operation plants are set up in various locations, but the founder is still in the headquarters.

As the company grows, communication becomes more siloed, and security controls are put in place to prevent knowledge from leaving the company. The same security controls block people in the company from sharing information that would help them make better decisions. This marks the end of sales and operations sitting together and the beginning of a very siloed business. For the past 20 years, Oliver Wright highlighted collaborative business planning as a best practice that demanded that companies go back to putting business functions in the same room, and back to sharing important information, resulting in significant performance gains. To make this happen we need actionable intelligence.

What Is Collaborative Business Planning?

Collaborative business planning is a regularly executed process that brings all business function plans into one integrated plan that is reviewed by the management from an aggregate level. It reconciles demand and supply plans at detail and aggregate level and links to the operating plan. The process usually covers the business plans over an 18-month horizon to help with the allocation of resources and the execution of business plans and strategy.

Aligning all of a company's plans nets some very significant results. Most important, it will make the company much more efficient by making management responsible for reconciling all the different plans and optimizing the different goals in the company for the best end result. This efficiency can result in shorter lead times, less stock-outs, better forecasts, and less excess inventory. See Table 6.1 for sample benefits.

Table 6.1   Sample Efficiency Benefits

Operation Area	% Change Range	Median
On-time delivery to customers	+10–40%	+25%
Inventory levels	−12–70%	−41%
Manufacturing downtime	−20–50%	−35%
Plant efficiency	+2–33%	+17%
Transportation costs	−5–30%	−17%

SOURCE: Tom Wallace, "Sales & Operations Planning: Costs and Benefits: The Financial View of Implementing Executive S&OP," T. F. Wallace & Company (2009): 6.

These are benefits reported by 13 major companies implementing collaborative business planning according to a T. F. Wallace study on sales and operations planning benefits in 2009. Another major benefit worth mentioning is the increase in forecast accuracy. Because this process requires more information from all parties, the forecasting model becomes more robust. In the same study, there was a forecast error reduction of 20 to 25 percent. As a touchstone, Figure 6.1 shows the required actions to support collaborative business planning (CBP). This does not have to be complex, but it does need to be fast and results-oriented. Each day your organization isn't achieving effective-CBP results is another day competitors gain an edge.

It is not all smooth sailing once you start. Here are some challenges this business process entails:

- Naming a champion or expert to lead the implementation
- Obtaining senior management support

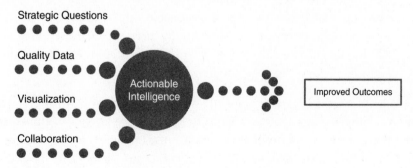

Figure 6.1   Key Requirements for Actionable Intelligence to Make a Difference

- Achieving process compliance
- Proper definition, understanding, and acceptance of assigned roles and responsibilities including the identification of the specific objectives for employee appraisals
- Establishing collaborative meetings as a business priority
- Establishing IT-enabled processes with adequate tool functionality

All in all, these bullet points are very similar to the needed factors for actionable intelligence. Companies need to build the right technologies, adapt their processes to the new capabilities, and get the support of management to ensure the project is adopted and carried out properly.

Linking Collaboration to Actionable Intelligence

Enabling collaboration among business functions with actionable intelligence is a bit of a chicken-and-egg story. Which one comes first is always a problem, but, in the end, the same results will be achieved. Once one is in place, it will be a relatively small step to institute the other.

- **From collaboration to actionable intelligence:** If actionable intelligence capabilities will be delivered when collaboration processes are already instated, this will open a new world to each function's users. By delivering answers to questions and in-depth views on the business situation, your actionable intelligence capabilities can greatly enhance the collaboration meetings. Now the users can have meetings that are more fact-based, thus making the company more efficient.
- **From actionable intelligence to collaboration:** Actionable intelligence makes the step to effective collaboration very small. It is mostly a process that builds on top of actionable intelligence, so to come up with collaborative business planning after you delivered actionable intelligence could even be a logical next step in enhancing the decision-making process of management.

Of course, the synergies delivered will work both ways. Collaboration allows companies to achieve actionable intelligence as well as embed it into their business and improve actionable intelligence. It is an escalating, collaborating effect. In the process of integrating collaborative business planning with actionable intelligence we can discern four stages:

Stage 1: Improved communications. At this first stage, data is incomplete and requires verification, and other issues are unresolved as yet, but a calendar and cadence have been established.

Stage 2: Problem solving. There are still problems in the process, but data for decision making is more trustworthy and problems are more visible and can be actively addressed.

Stage 3: Problem prevention. Near-term problems have been addressed, allowing the management team to focus its attention further ahead into the future planning horizon.

Stage 4: Strategic and tactical decision making. Collaborative business planning is a mature process and now the company has solidly implemented problem solving and prevention. The management team closes gaps between the reality of the situation and its alignment with business goals.

Ground Zero

The start of integrating collaborative business planning with actionable intelligence is usually recognizable by an announcement that sales and operations planning (S&OP) is being implemented, followed by some skepticism from departments around the company and top management. Sales and operations' best-practice leaders and gurus always claim that fact-based decision making has to be led from the top, because that is the only way to get groups that were siloed—and may even have a dysfunctional relationship—to sit in the same room with each other. But they miss an important point. Many business function leaders make a business of protecting data and massaging it so their department looks good. Getting them to share this data with each other requires a senior leader to come in and insist on full transparency—and accept no other alternative.

By providing full transparency we can also create actionable intelligence. When a company embarks on the process of collaborating, it should at the same time enable actionable intelligence capabilities, leading to full transparency.

Stage 1: Improved communications can be achieved by showing each department what can be gained. The "what's in it for me" question should be addressed, not just with words, but by showing how making data reliable and sharing reliable data can make a world of difference. It also opens dialogue between departments and eventually cultivates trust between them.

Stage 2: Problem solving is an important first step toward planning sales and operations. Start by bringing departments together to clear the problems that inhibit the sharing of the individual units' plans. Addressing these problems creates a common goal to work toward and makes the roadblocks visible. This will start to get purposeful at this point, and actionable intelligence has the power to be the backbone of visualizing problems in different plans by completing, validating, and visualizing the plans themselves.

Stage 3: Problem prevention is enabled by supply and demand alignment on a forward planning horizon appropriate for the business. After all, for problem prevention you need forward visibility. Aligning for the next year or the next two years allows companies to map the challenges in getting the right goods to the right place at the right time. It's important to get product-level details by location—especially price, costs, and quantity—because these help set the priority for resource allocation, which is the main principle of collaboration. In Stage 3, actionable intelligence will provide the collaborative business planning meeting with the details it needs to get that overarching plan together. It isn't possible to have an effective collaboration without actionable intelligence.

Stage 4: Strategic and tactical decision making is only possible when actionable intelligence has been established alongside collaboration at a global, regional, and local level. It's about optimizing the entire company. Many companies make the mistake of optimizing just portions of themselves, where the data is cleaner, and where the support is more pronounced. But in doing so, they may optimize one part and in the process deoptimize many others. This becomes apparent when they run through the business scorecard and realize that there are trade-offs between, for example, high customer service, inventory, and shipping costs. The deeper work to establish relationships between the KPIs has to be done before the benefits can be fully achieved at Stage 4.

The benefits of arriving at Stage 4 include truly being able to set targets in an optimal way, which sometimes surprisingly means reducing targets in one area to accelerate targets in another area. By focusing the organization on an optimized model and putting aside the traditional KPIs that were being approved without a thorough understanding of the impact, the business can achieve better performance and consistently allocate resources in the right way.

A Continuing Challenge

Take note, this is not a one-time effort. As business challenges emerge, or growth opportunities appear, actionable intelligence capabilities need to be further improved and the model revised for nimble reactions to stakeholder needs. The best example of this is when there is a jolt or catastrophe in the economy. With economic models, a company can see whether the business might turn down, but it might not be clear what products and services will be impacted most or least. As a result, it is not clear what manufacturing capability or distribution capacity will be needed. This lack of information creates a very bumpy ride and leads to missed earnings calls, senior management turnover, and poor morale.

If leaders do not make fundamental changes and adjust their strategies and tactics, the organization simply flounders. Alternatively, by collaborating across business functions connected to the economic situation, competitors, customers, and suppliers, using big data we can drill into the specific SKUs and brands that could be impacted. Based on our future plans and actionable intelligence we can predict where sales will occur, how much cash we need to tie up in inventory, and what opportunities we need to seek to improve margins by selling products that have a better margin with a lower cost basis. During lean times companies can't make mistakes selling the wrong products with the wrong costs at the wrong price. However, companies with poor KPIs that drive the wrong behavior end up doing just that.

It is imperative that companies connect their end-to-end value chains in order to support the best outcomes. Once they have achieved that they must engage in enabling even more and better actionable intelligence.

Collaborative Business Planning Health Check

To ensure your process is working well, here is a quick health check for the company. By answering these questions truthfully you can find out where there could be breakpoints and bottlenecks in the process.

✓ Does your regular cadence of activities involve senior leadership?
✓ Does the executive summary bring to life the situation and consider the internal and external situations?
✓ Instead of just telling stories, are you showing facts?
✓ Do you review an action register and is each action aligned with improving KPIs and answering strategic business questions?

✓ Are proactive decisions made?

✓ Are you using forward-looking KPIs?

✓ Does the process cover all major areas of the business for the next 18 months or an appropriate planning horizon?

✓ At preparation meetings are all business units able to review the same data?

✓ Is there a financial view dashboard that allows easy access to drill into information at a product and service level with granular details ?

✓ Are discrepancies between the business plan and the financial plan evaluated monthly?

✓ Does it occur on a monthly cycle?

✓ Does it include a capacity review?

✓ Does it include actual versus forecasted sales?

✓ Are accountabilities clearly defined?

In the end, succeeding in collaborative business planning can be a challenging project of its own, a journey almost as interesting as the one delivering actionable intelligence. Though truth be told, actionable intelligence is a foundational element of collaborative business planning, and they can really complement each other by having similar requirements and a similar process. The hard benefits of properly implementing both can transform the business, and the soft benefits are simply priceless.

However, implementing either project is not free and nobody has unlimited resources. Therefore, we also need governance of the actionable intelligence project.

Summary and Considerations

Point to Ponder: Collaboration between business functions and across regions will deliver tremendous value.

Quote to Remember: "Business leaders have made careers out of massaging data."

Question to Consider: What common strategic business question could be sponsored by a senior leader and bring people from across the company to deliver actionable intelligence?

Chapter 7

Governance: Funding Intelligence, Protecting the Results

Key Points and Questions

- Governance should be a facilitator of communication, priority, and oversight. If it's seen as a block or a hassle, it's broken. . . . fix it. Like a referee, the best project managers are in the middle of the game, but not noticeable except when needed.
- Governance's biggest responsibility should be to review past projects for the business results achieved. This is the only way to validate new business cases.
- Change the mindset from one of risk avoidance to seizing opportunity, and governance will be established correctly and deliver:

  - Insights during crisis with all stakeholders

  - Faster view on capability to leverage competitor mistakes

  - Appropriate pricing of goods and services

- Never use the term "postmortem" on a project, unless you really want it dead. When a project is delivered, that's when the most important support for adoption and benefits capture begins!
- Definitely use post-governance for intelligence projects!
- Tighten security. Secure your newfound strategic insights by classifying data and reducing access to a need-to-know basis. Anything connected to the Internet is up for grabs by hackers. Take your most critical data offline.

An Actionable Intelligence Governance Methodology

Actionable intelligence should be lightly governed, quickly delivered, and heavily used.

If you are the leader governing projects or a professional pitching a project, here are some key performance indicators (KPIs) you need to consider:

- What is the situation today?
- What should it be?
- How to improve it?
- Who needs to improve it?
- How will they be compensated for improving it? Is it a simple pat on the back or it is an increase in salary?

I'm so frustrated with our governance process, we should scrap it and start it all over again.

—Senior business executives, most companies, most places in the world

A governance model provides a blueprint for how a company decides to manage its resources to fund projects that would provide the best return on investment, are best aligned to support the strategy, and have the highest likelihood of success. The final goal of pitching projects for the project's leader is twofold. First, you want your project to be accepted by the business leaders so you can start. Second, you want them to give you a budget to work with.

To objectively assess whether a project has a high or a low chance of being accepted by management, put yourself in management's shoes and ask yourself: What should a project aim to deliver for you to be able to accept it? Would you say it fits into the company's strategy? Now think of how the actionable intelligence projects fit into that criterion. Would they be accepted?

Note here that I see every iteration of actionable intelligence as a separate project. Every time you answer a new strategic business question for a new sponsor, get a new budget and a new review of the results. This is what "govern lightly" means, and it is also the approach that results in the highest chance of acceptance for your first project. Think of it this way: management would much rather spend a small sum, so run a low risk, than be confronted with a giant budget application. If you apply for one small project at a time, you can much more easily show fast results to support starting up the next. Due to the synergies of the individual actionable intelligence projects, total costs for these projects tend to go up linearly or even become cheaper, while the results grow exponentially.

An excellent intelligence governance model will give money now and ask questions later!

Now I will show what to keep in mind when going through the governance of your projects.

Before you start, bear in mind that for our project of actionable intelligence against all the other projects, leaders need to adhere to three main concepts:

1. Not all categories of projects should be governed in the same way.
2. Every project should have a measurement for success.
3. There should be a methodology for fast-tracking projects.

Unlike Table 7.1, which displays different levels of engagement based on the category of project, the typical project management process has only one methodology that engages all involved regardless of the project. The management process starts off with the registration of a new project, then continues with finding a business sponsor who will support it with a budget for the project's execution, actually executes the project, and concludes with a review. There are three project categories: (1) intelligence, (2) infrastructure, and (3) fast-track unbudgeted. The first category consists of intelligence projects that are projects involving mostly intellectual change but usually

Table 7.1   Governance Applied Selectively Based on Project Category

Project Category

	PMO*	Sponsor	Budget	Execution	Review Results
Intelligence	Register	✓	✓	✓	✓
Infrastructure	Register	✓	✓	✓	✓
Fast-track intelligence	Skip	✓	Skip	✓	✓ And budget

*Project Management Office.

no big investment in capital to sponsor tangible results, as the deliverable is intelligence.

Normally, intelligence projects will be registered and approved, as are all the projects. Then the tasks of getting a sponsor, budget, and execution will be fast and easily checked before reaching the ultimate goal of the review.

The second type of project will be infrastructure projects, aimed at delivering tangibles like machines and equipment. Compared to the fast checks of intelligence projects, these are typically slow processes whereby the person in charge at every stage will review before passing to the next stage.

The third category is fast-track unbudgeted. As its name suggests, this is very similar to an intelligence project with fast-process approvals, except that there are no allocated intelligence budgets granted, and it goes straight from getting a business sponsor to execution and then to review. During the review phase, the results are monetized and compared against the amount of budget ultimately used.

Methodology for Fast-Tracking Projects

Whenever business leaders become frustrated with the slow pace of governance they start to look for ways to shortcut the approval process. This becomes clear when invoices show up without purchase orders or vendors are placed in the system without due diligence or budgets used without prior approval. Typically there are several symptoms:

- There are several approval levels that are difficult to get past, but that actually never say "no" in the end. They just ask a lot of questions, annoy the heck out of you, and add no value to the validation process . . . but they've always done it and have made a career out of it so live with it!

- The paperwork to fill out for a project is onerous and doesn't actually provide clarity on the measurable benefits.
- Governance meetings bring lots of people together but little gets done and everyone leaves unsatisfied with the outcome, because no one comes prepared. Everyone in the meeting is reading the documentation, so comments become subjective, confused, and of little value.
- There exists lack of clarity on who can actually approve a project. This is especially true in multinational companies. Is the money being spent locally? Does the region need to approve? Is the impact global? Does corporate need to approve? The favorite one is when a local organization wants to use a new, cool software tool, but corporate IT doesn't have it as a standard. Who gets to approve—the business leaders or IT?

All these and more cause IT governance to fail miserably . . . but there's hope! Simply remove the "yes men," clarify the ownership of benefit delivery, and finally make sure the results can be measured.

Introducing "post-governance," a fast-track model for intelligence projects. To validate that the project qualifies, we ask a series of questions:

- Is this an actionable intelligence project or something else?
  - If this is an actionable intelligence project, then confirm with the sponsors the measure of success and review their past performance in delivering success. If both are good, then execute.
  - If this is another type of project, confirm there is a budget.
    - If there is a budget, then confirm what is the measure of success with the sponsors and review their past performance in delivering success. If both are good, then execute.
    - If no budget exists, wait for next budget round for approval.
- Is there an Accountable Consulted, Execution (ACE) chart with one single "yes" in each role so it is very clear?

By using the ACE chart (Table 7.2) to clearly outline the accountabilities and measurements up front, the governance model becomes much faster, and the goal of communicating the types of projects that are going on is still achieved.

Table 7.2 Accountable, Consulted, Execution Chart for Projects

	Accountable	Consulted	Execution
Business manager and team			Yes
IT leader and team			Yes
Business sponsor	Yes		
Other business units and IT leaders		Yes	
C-level		Yes	

Accountable as the business sponsor, he/she uses the capabilities delivered by the project to improve business results.

Consulted: This two-way communication ensures everyone is on the right page but doesn't slow down progress. It allows peers and seniors to have their say and be engaged in the project. Engagement enables team work and promotes support for the project.

Execution team members make the project happen.

Note, this assumes three things:

1. There is an agreed-upon strategy that everyone is working toward.
2. There are agreed-upon KPIs that support the strategy.
3. There are approved budgets that can be used for the projects (except for actionable intelligence, which is self-funding).

Whoa, actionable intelligence is self-funding? Yes, if you've followed the model in this book you will achieve far more savings than it costs. All you need is a budget to get the first pieces of actionable intelligence started to answer the first strategic business questions. However, if you don't follow the model, you will fail and be fired, and your firing will fund the project. So even though actionable intelligence is not funded, you still need to deliver. Unofficially allocated resources, like man-hours, are also a form of funding. You still have to spend them wisely and deliver on the project goals.

One winter morning, Estée Lauder's head of IT development and I met at Starbucks to lay out how we would work together. We brought a vendor along as a mediator. We had ownership and communication challenges across our teams as well as mixed expectations regarding who would deliver what. By meeting, we were able to draw lines that gave us much more solid footing and enabled us to work together well for the next several years.

Governing Does Not Stop with Approving

When fast-tracking or in the regular governing path, you will come to a point where your project is approved and you reach the execution phase. During this execution stage of the project, governance is most importantly good communications. Managing the actionable intelligence project well means telling your boss what you are up to, regardless of whether this is your first actionable intelligence project or your 15th.

Governing the project is not always smooth sailing; you could run into problems like these:

- Data acquisition can be unexpectedly difficult.
- Iterative development of visualizations can require more iterations, or fewer, depending on user imagination, needs, and capabilities.
- Scope can change rapidly as benefits are captured and shown in one area, which results in additional work. Normally, "pre-governance" really slows down the project, because the additional spend requires rejustification through governance boards and so on.

To be successful, a high level of communication about what is being done and the priorities of the projects in the queue is needed to set expectations. Again, keep the business sponsors engaged. Not only will you keep their attention and stay top-of-mind, you will also build their trust in you and subsequently their continued support of your project.

The project does not end once the company has implemented the business intelligence tool. Leaders and teams need to make sure the process is usable and workable; if not, the project is not going to succeed and all the effort and money spent will be wasted. In fact, a survey by SAS showed that only 12 percent of data management professionals had actually implemented a big data strategy, because most of them don't understand it, don't understand the benefits, or do not have the necessary support.[1]

Every Project Should Have a Measurement for Success

What have the IT projects we approved delivered to us?

—A Fortune 500 chief financial officer

With this one question, thousands of hours of IT work and thousands more hours of governance of the IT work were challenged. There weren't any good, well-documented answers.

Most IT projects are considered hard to measure because they are part of improving execution efficiency. How can the benefits of the project be separated from the benefits of business performance, the external environment, and other mitigating circumstances?

It can be done and it must be done to answer a savvy CFO's question, but the problem doesn't belong in the lap of IT. You know what I am going to say next: It is the business sponsor who needs to set the measurement and be accountable for the results.

Earlier in the book we linked collaborative business performance with financial performance. So it is also possible to link project performance to overall business performance. Before the project gets approved, leaders need to think through the following: What are the impacts? What are the soft benefits? And what are the hard benefits? After the project is completed, make sure that both soft and hard benefits have been derived from the project before any further money is invested. The results have to justify the investment spending.

Once you have committed to the benefits to be achieved, you are now able to measure the results. While you execute the IT project, keep in view how the project will be measured and make sure the business process, training for people, and technology will enable the measurement.

For intelligence projects, the achievement of the goal is the most important indicator of success. The challenge is that the goals are often very soft, such as:

- React quickly to changes in the business environment with actionable intelligence.
- Protect customer value by meeting their needs based on social media with actionable intelligence.
- Avoid loss by performing a thorough risk management assessment with actionable intelligence.
- Understand what the best outcomes could be based on current planning.
- Reduce the amount of time and e-mails needed to come to consensus about the current situation.

Each of these are measurable. Here are some comments we received from business users at companies that have applied the lessons from this book:

"An ad campaign caused a 50 percent increase in the forecast. We have weekly discussions with demand planning, materials planning, and resource planning about supporting this growth—a significant forecast increase compared to three months ago, worth $2.23 million. We're coming to the table with actionable intelligence to discuss; what do we need to build towards?"—Leading cosmetics manufacturer

"By linking social media tweets from our consumers into the customer service department we were able to respond to tweets about discontinued and hard-to-find products, setting the consumers' expectations. Sometimes we saved sales by shipping the product especially to the customer"—Online shoe retailer

"Our end-to-end visibility during the Japan crisis was magic! We identified the entire sales and supply chain risk on the same day, and we were able to make specific contingencies based on facts."—Crisis management team member at a consumer products company

"We've been conducting inventory evaluation with corporate business intelligence and supply chain to understand why inventory for a specific brand has increased so dramatically over the past year. Using actionable intelligence, we were able to identify the root cause of leftover pieces after a project was completed, worth $27,000 in excess. It's a good example that we need to align and have process defined for any demand changes to limited life products. We're now working on hammering out best practices and how to foster more dialog in the global supply chain."—Leading fast-moving consumer goods (FMCG) supply planning lead

"I used to have to wait for days to know whether we would have enough product to meet a retailer's increased demand. Now I can simply look at our global actionable intelligence and the discussion instantly starts with, 'May I have some of the inventory?'"—Country-level sales team member at an FMCG company

As you can see, every project can be measured by its value and tracked for performance, thus justifying the spend. This is why actionable intelligence projects can be fast-tracked and reviewed after the fact.

Doing so makes both the business and IT accountable for delivering business results. For IT, tie the success of past and current projects to future funding and bonuses to make the linkage very clear. By doing this you will raise the morale of the IT department, because they will be able to show tangible successes of their work.

Governance Does Not Stop with Results Either

The methodology of post-governance ensures the actionable intelligence project start and finish quickly and the results are weighed against the costs. Measuring benefits and costs shows the real usefulness of the project and builds trust for upcoming projects. This allows the team to move fast on answering the strategic business question, because new approvals will be received for setting up actionable intelligence projects for new questions.

Even if you have booked one success, you still need the right follow-through to guarantee the second project's success will follow automatically. Here are some pointers to keep in mind as to how you should follow up on the first iteration of actionable intelligence:

- Prioritize the work with the senior leadership team to ensure you are working on the hottest strategic business questions. By focusing on the strategic questions you ensure senior management is backing you up and trusts you will deliver. It also provides you with some pressure, so be warned. After a project is done, you should go back to senior leadership, both to prove the results and to get the next strategic business question.
- A business sponsor is required for each actionable intelligence capability. They do not just provide project development funding but also post-development funding. Just donating funding to start up the project is not enough to keep it alive. You will need money to upgrade the project to the current business need and to provide training in the long run, too.
- Post-govern by reviewing the usage of the new capabilities. If it's not being used, or the quality isn't there, then dig in to find root cause, and make the appropriate changes in either the intelligence team or the business team. Results are born from usage, so this is an important next step.

- Work with sponsors and supporters who have a clear vision of how intelligence will be used and have the power to ensure you have the data you need to make it come alive.

In practical terms, when using the results of the first project to determine the requirements for the second, keep in mind that each project is different. A great approach here would be combining the information you have, namely the output of ideation sessions, as well as the results from your first iteration(s) of iterative development of actionable intelligence. People can help you decide what should be required outside of the benchmark of your first project. The added bonus is that this practice basically eliminates the need for the project charters and pre-governance approvals normally required during software development.

In short: Governance starts with getting the instant approval for the actionable intelligence project and continues with you monitoring the project, documenting the results, and delivering these documented results when you apply for a new actionable intelligence project. You post-govern by assessing the way actionable intelligence is used and the results it delivered.

Governance and post-governance only work if you have enough money to work with on the right budget lines. To that end, we take a closer look at the budgeting aspect.

Intelligence Budgeting

Every project costs money, even creating actionable intelligence capabilities. So the actionable intelligence project should also be budgeted properly. You do not want to be halfway through your project, hit some roadblock, and find your money is used up. So it is time to convince the business sponsors to give you enough to work with in order to be able to deliver. You might even ask for leeway to overspend ... or just do it and ask for forgiveness later.

There are a number of reasons why most intelligence budgets are rarely exposed to the public:

1. It is difficult to explain why the budget is what it is. Because it is rapid and iterative, it's very difficult to estimate how much a budget should be.
2. The results of actionable intelligence are sometimes embarrassing and at other times frightening, so you can only share so much of it.

3. No one would believe the tremendous benefits actionable intelligence provides until they see it for themselves.
4. The data clean-up work is always harder than expected and requires funding for work that is normally considered the jobs people are paid to do.

Nevertheless, to get a budget you should be able to sell the project. So think of it the following way:

The usual questions you'll face: How much does it cost? What is the benefit? To be honest, you probably will have no idea—absolutely no clue. You could quote similar projects, but each one will be different.

But asking those two questions is the same thing as asking: What is the cost of food? And what is the benefit? To someone in a developing country it might cost three days' labor to make enough money for a decent meal. Whereas in developed countries people have already earned enough to pay for their meal by the time the morning coffee break arrives. Would it make sense to ask for the cost and benefit of the food for these two different situations? No! People in both situations need to eat to survive. And whatever the cost, it's worth the benefit, especially in the long run. You can go without food for a day or two but not for months, even if its costs outweigh its perceived direct benefits.

Remember the Key Points of the UPS Story

For actionable intelligence roughly the same holds. In the long run, and I cannot stress this enough, each and every one benefits. In the long run, competitors with the capabilities will have the edge over companies without any actionable intelligence. To overcome the budgeting challenge, here are my three recommendations for budgeting for actionable intelligence:

1. Start small and conservative. The effort needs to grow like Google did, slowly, keeping costs low, and delivering results to key team members. Your main challenges will be:
- Usage and buy-in by the business users
- Stakeholder support
- Capturing demonstrated results
- Access to accurate data

No amount of money can help capture these points faster, but with some good old-fashioned patience and perseverance, you will get the desired results. Furthermore, you will need money for this to start up:

- The right small team composed of corporate stakeholder, data acquisition, visualization, and change management needs to be in place.
- Implement a temporary central data repository that you fully control.
- Acquire a data visualization tool like QlikView with enough client access licenses for your team, boss, stakeholders, and a few more to spare. You'll need them.

2. **Build fast.**
   - Establish a baseline for data support and data acquisition expense.
   - Bring in a consulting team that can visualize quickly. Invest in that quantitative whiz who creates fast algorithms. Invest in a business analyst to deliver great visualizations to answer business questions.
   - Buy ready-to-use visualization tools like the QlikView tools mentioned in this book.

3. **Create intelligence capabilities as a shared service.**
   - Ensure the intelligence organization is funded by the core function where it started plus external functions so you can have some objective use of funds. This also ensures the stakeholders' money is good for their requests.
   - Insist on training and support budgets as well as travel and expenses for your evangelist so the value of actionable intelligence can be shared far and wide.

In following these principles, you will have a framework to get the budget to deliver actionable intelligence. Now all you need is cost justification, which you develop by dividing your budget over the different budget categories.

Key Budget Categories

This is a list of the resources and capabilities needed to sustain an actionable intelligence organization. It is modeled after the Central Intelligence Agency organization and budget.[2] Then it was tweaked for a corporate environment and the need to achieve high adoption and monetize results.

Core Capabilities   Provide data acquisition resources for constant testing and data acquisition. No need to have an actionable intelligence system if you can't deliver the data accurately and in a timely fashion. This requires funding. The intelligence stops working if this aspect is not 100 percent accurate all the time.

Technology   The right technology at the right scale, at the right time. Actionable intelligence is not big data, where "build a bigger mousetrap and they will come" applies. Users do not care about the cloud and huge data warehouses. They want answers, now. Start small and focus the dollars on intelligence and answers. Then, as the user engagement increases, build the technology infrastructure to match. It is a responsible way to deliver IT.

We all know faster technology becomes cheaper quickly, so why invest in big, cool systems when they become slow and cheap soon after a purchase? Start with just the power you need and scale quickly.

During our project, the breaking point for governance was when the IT department asked how many CPU cycles I would need so they could spec out a server—at the beginning of the project. We simply couldn't hazard a guess. Instead, we used some decommissioned servers and set up a parallel processing configuration. As we grew, we simply added more servers in parallel. It worked, fast, cheap, and scaled with growing requirements. Remember, speed is critical to success.

Change Management   Definitely have a very good change management team and change management approach. You should overspend and overdo change management. You need to provide more support than you expect: help-desk information, online documentation, and so on. Go to the users' desks.

When I first started at Estée Lauder I was inspired by the legend of the founder, Joseph Lauder, "walking the floor" to check on how the people in the company were faring. Every project I've seen succeed has this as a component. It is often overlooked and cut when the project is delivered, but, in fact, this is the most important part.

Imagine a world where Fast Moving Consumer Goods (FMCG) companies made a product, placed it in the warehouse and on the shelves, and then just stopped. No support, no advertising, that's it. The products wouldn't sell to expectations, right? But this is the model of many business intelligence projects. There's even that word "postmortem"—why call a project dead when it is just beginning?

This budget line is a critical and ongoing component to the success of actionable intelligence.

For proven success, follow my Sustainable Training Model. It just works. (See the model in Chapter 8.)

Also, establish a culture in which people are rewarded for both creating best practices as well as adopting best practices.

Travel and Expenses   Participation at business unit and regional meetings is part of the walk-the-floor methodology mentioned earlier. The in-person presence helps the actionable intelligence team assess where there are needs and understand directly from the users how the intelligence will be used.

Putting these budget lines in place with agreed-upon flexibility from the senior sponsor keeps the delivery organization in place for the long-term and makes it as exciting as possible for the analysts.

This list is a good place to start. To stretch your dollars, confirm the application of capital versus expenses with your finance department.

Governing the Use of Actionable Intelligence and Establishing Data Security

Governance is not just about managing the funds and budgets in the right way. Sometimes, it requires the selection of the right projects to achieve regulatory compliance and sometimes the wrong analyses are made, leading to the wrong projects being picked. Those projects may then lead to a damaged reputation.

In the United States, for example, intelligence is used in law enforcement where agents track activity on social media platforms to determine whether there is a chance of an upcoming riot or a threat. This is supported by reports about a National Security Agency project known as PRISM whereby the U.S. and British governments have been requesting information from nine U.S. companies, including Facebook, Google, Apple, and Microsoft.[3]

As a result of this revelation about the government, the public has expressed concern about their use of such services due to fear of privacy leaks. This can be a cause for concern for companies like Google, whose business models rely on customer trust.

But notice that the public use of cell phones, e-mail, and social media has continued to grow in spite of the intrusion on privacy.

The backstory, which isn't being covered, is how governments and commercial entities are using this intelligence to spy on commercial entities to:

- Gain insider knowledge ahead of public announcements
- Know about plans and new business models
- Position themselves to take advantage

If a 20-something-year-old has access to intelligence and shows it to a newspaper as did Eric Snowden, how many more young people in positions to retrieve commercial information use it for financial gain?

This brings to mind the question of how intelligence should be used.

For Better, for Worse

There is always more than one way to do something. It all depends on what is valued. Should we make a decision that would ensure the long-term greater good of people, or should the decision be made based on the short-term gains? Similar decisions must be made regarding the use of intelligence. Should intelligence be used to improve the welfare of employees, or should it be used to limit the use of employee benefits?

I once came across a company where they used business intelligence the wrong way. They used their business intelligence capabilities to track whether employees were using the lower or higher cost option for their health care choice. The audit showed that there were branches where employees used the more expensive option on a regular basis. The corporate office used that data to reprimand management in those branches and made them set a target use number for the cheaper alternative. A year later, that target had been achieved, and the company saved money. However, decreasing the health care services that a company promised to its employees at the time of hiring doesn't seem a good use of this intelligence. A better method would have been to:

- Show the more expensive health care providers that they were receiving more business and renegotiate the contracts.
- Analyze the reasons for the health care usage and then spend money to educate that office about prevention or healthy lifestyles that

would have a double positive effect of reducing days off and improving morale through better health.

- Understand the causes and predispositions of various common illnesses to ensure new employees are screened and, if hired, educated as part of their employment agreement to ensure that they take the necessary and appropriate steps to protect themselves.

Make the right call when deciding how you use your business intelligence capabilities. It will leave an impact on your journey, be it via team morale or company reputation.

Google Cheat View

In 2009 a woman filed for a divorce from her husband after looking at the street view of Google Maps. She recognized her husband's Range Rover at her female friend's house when the husband was supposed to be away on business. Other similar examples include a man being caught leaving a sex shop while another was caught smoking under a no smoking sign.[4]

To the public this can be alarming, since it feels as if your every move and action is being watched. In reality, these images tend to be static pictures that will not be updated for several years. However, Big Brother is always watching us.

Today, Google provides an app called Google Now. It allows you to, for free, track your location and archive where you went every day and night. This data can be exported and analyzed. If a company registered its company phones into this app, the employees could be seen, let's say, on their "sick day" to confirm their location is at the infirmary and not the horse racetrack.

The availability of data doesn't automatically mean it should be used. Make sure to deliver on the strategic business questions. This should provide enough purpose-driven work without diving into employees lives intrusively.

Safety First

Your whole life is on the Internet, and it might be used against you.

Safe Internetbanking ran a campaign in Brussels, Belgium, featuring a "mind reader" named Dave.[5] Unsuspecting individuals were invited into a tent and told that Dave would be reading their minds. Dave was able to reveal personal information about the motorcycles they owned, the butterfly tattoos on their lower backs, the schools or homes that they study or live in. More incredibly, he was able to reveal what they had spent money on, their bank account numbers, and how much they had in their accounts.

During the big reveal when the screens came down, viewers could see a team of individuals with computers and large screens googling various websites to provide Dave with all the information he needed to convince people that he was a mind reader.

In this day and age the Internet is so accessible that it makes it easy for individuals to obtain information about us. The threat is out there, and we need to be protecting ourselves.

Protect the Hard Work

If our personal data can be accessed by these malignant individuals, then what about the project we worked so hard on creating? Data security is important to your project, rather, it is essential. You cannot build an advantage with your actionable intelligence if the public at large or your major competitors are accessing the same intelligence. So data security is not only important, it is essential.

Many people working with data have no idea how important it is to protect it. Those who do have an idea how valuable security is usually don't know the facts; they believe the myths. They believe they are safe. This is the same fallacy that actually got you on the road to actionable intelligence, remember? No facts, just myths.

Oracle released a paper that dispelled some of the myths about data security:[6]

Myth: Hackers cause most security breaches.
In fact, 80 percent of data loss is caused by insiders.

Myth: Encryption makes your data secure.
In fact, encryption is only one approach to securing data. Security also requires access control, data integrity, system availability, and auditing.

Myth: Firewalls make your data secure.
In fact, 40 percent of Internet break-ins occur in spite of a firewall being in place.

I hope this has convinced you personally to take data security seriously, even if your company already has measures in place. I encourage you to think critically about the data security of your brainchild. I will not treat you to the hows of data security; that is outside the scope of this book. But here are a few widely touted security methods that don't work.

Data Security That Doesn't Work

- Supposedly superstrong passwords that don't provide context for the user to remember them. These end up on Post-it notes stuck to the computer.
- Passwords that expire every 90 days. These end up on Post-it notes, too, and increase help desk tickets.
- Blocking senior management's access to data or taking weeks or months to provide it ends up making the IT department look bad.
- Blocking access for political reasons. This quickly becomes patently obvious and ends up making the person doing the blocking look petty.

Those approaches don't work well because people need to access data to do their work. When the wrong barrier to entry is put in place, users create work-arounds or establish bad habits. Or worse, they simply do not adopt the new capabilities. Security is a culture, not just a lock, and it requires a mentality of security to be ingrained into everyday activities.

Encounter with an Alleged Russian FSB Agent

While I was on a speedboat going from Phuket to James Bond Island for a tour, I met a man who wore a Yankees cap and spoke with a Russian accent. As the boat sped past idyllic scenery, he took out a long cigarette and started smoking at the back of the boat by the engine. I noticed that there was a certain unique hardness to him unlike any I had encountered in others. We discussed U.S., African, and local politics. At one point, he revealed to me that he was an ex-FSB agent. The FSB is the principal security agency of the Russian Federation and the main successor agency to the USSR's Committee of State Security (KGB). Its main responsibilities are within the country and include counterintelligence, internal and border security, counterterrorism, and surveillance, as well as investigating various other types of grave crimes.[7]

He had worked in Africa, and his job was to convince U.S. CIA agents to become double agents for Russia. At the same time he knew that others were attempting to do the same thing to Russian spies.

In talking with John Ritchie, ex-CIA agent, and now managing director of Global Security and Investigations at a global financial institution, I learned that convincing people to share what they know is part of the business of intelligence gathering.

How much information do you share with the key members on your intelligence team? How do you prevent them from turning against you and sharing the actionable intelligence that you have created with your competitors?

If I flew to Thailand, passed through immigrations where I would be highlighted as an American, used my cell phone to reserve a hotel room, and later used the hotel phone to book a tour, anyone with the access to data at these points will be able to use actionable intelligence and acquire the human intelligence about me.

Here is where we bring in big data. In 2012, the German Interior Minister Hans-Peter Friedrich acknowledged that the German police and intelligence had been sending 44,000 SMS messages to determine where people were located.[8] Had this or the GPS tracking been monitored in real time, the crime would have been prevented by:

- Observing where the cell phone of the policeman went during the day of the murders and how that matched the location of the cell phones of the victims.
- Linking the thefts at the safe-deposit box with cell phone monitoring to the policeman or one level deeper where the policeman's contact was in the area committing the crime and reporting success or failure.
- Highlighting that the location of the policeman at the time of the murders was unusual as an interview in an open, unsolved case would have generated some paperwork.

Everyone on Security Detail

From a security perspective, the Human Resources (HR) department, physical security team, and IT security team should all be engaged as soon as you publish actionable intelligence. The skill sets of employees in these three areas need to be upgraded so as to allow them to monitor, access, and mitigate risk of intelligence theft.

Everyone understands why the IT security team has to be on board, but the need for HR and physical security to be included may be less clear.

As you will read in Chapter 8, if HR has not done an analysis of current employees to determine whether any are exploitable or might already be violating the confidentiality agreement, it is time to make sure that happens. HR should have as part of its processes examining current communications and exploring big data about employees so as to uncover any illicit activity that might be going on.

The IT security team should be analyzing and capturing all data on the networks in the company. They should be analyzing internal communications to see if there are proscribed communications taking place. Should an individual be suspected of engaging in such activity, IT should check the following:

- Has the employee ever sent attachments to people outside the company and if so what was in the attachment?
- Did the employee use his USB to download company information?
- Are there encrypted entries on the employee's online calendar?
- Can IT use the company-provided cell phone to track where the employee has been?
- Is the employee friends with competitors or friends of friends of competitors (which should naturally be the case) on social media and are there any patterns of inappropriate information sharing occuring?
- Run a credit check and a net worth check of the employee and close family to see if there is any indication of money issues.

As for the physical security team, they have the necessary expertise to conduct the investigations, skill sets that the IT security team lacks. In addition, should there be any security breach, the physical security team will also provide the security lockdown of physical infrastructure in sync with any IT lockdown that the IT security team activates.

Spying on Your Intelligence Organization, the Most Important Work!

Intelligence organizations have the most information and the best insight into current and future business situations. Thus the individuals with access to this information become part of an elite and highly trusted class within the company. Together, they will know more ahead of time than all levels of management. It is imperative to have the right monitoring in place to prevent information leakage that would damage the company.

For example, recently there was a police officer who committed a double murder in Singapore. The facts of the case as reported by *The Straits Times* are as follows:

- The officer recently declared bankruptcy.
- One of the victims was an owner of a company and a private land owner indicating he had some wealth and means.
- The same victim had his safe-deposit box broken into last fall during a rash of break-ins at a secure location. No deeper police information about these break-ins was provided.
- This policeman had looked into the safe-deposit theft even though the case was not assigned to him.
- Early on the morning of the day of the murder, the victim emptied the safe-deposit box. He was murdered at his home that very day. His son was wounded and later died.

An officer with financial problems is privvy to intelligence about a wealthy crime victim. What could have been done to stop this crime?

Two Singapore telecom companies, Starhub and Singtel, acknowledged in the same newspaper that they keep track of cell phone locations in real time. In fact, in the famous 1997 case where a National Serviceman took an automatic weapon from his base to go find and kill his ex-girlfriend, his cell phone broadcast his position as he travelled through Singapore, and the police easily caught him and prevented the crime.

To prevent this crime from happening, the following controls should have been in place:

- All officers should register their net worth. In Singapore, this is dead easy. All salary payments are tracked by the Central Provident Fund and Inland Revenue Authority of Singapore and deducted automatically. The filing of Singapore taxes is a five-minute exercise: yes I made this much, yes I paid this much in rent/loans, yes these are my accounts, submit . . . done. So we have a full picture of the officer's financial position, but wait there's more.
- All bank accounts are already registered under the National Registration Identity Card (NRIC) so an individual's savings position, or lack thereof, plus all outstanding loans can be easily discovered.

With these two pieces of information we can project bankruptcy like a nine-year-old can add fractions.

We know the family birth certificates, insurance, and other registrations are also centrally kept by the employer. So the same analysis can be done across the family members who might be in a position to assist the individual.

Maybe a friend will help out? Enter, social media. Because every phone is registered to the NRIC as well as all home online accounts, all friends and family who he is connected to on social media can also be identified and investigated. After determining the net worth of these friends, it is easier to know if they can help. Answer found.

But just because he doesn't get any help, that's no cause to pick him up for a crime he hasn't committed, right?

None of this is rocket science; we don't need rock star, hard core data scientists to catch unusual, highly visible activity like this. Let us prevent the 80 percent of the crimes that are highly visible first, then invest in trying to predict the remaining 20 percent. Not the other way around.

Summary and Considerations

Point to Ponder: Post-governance emphasizes monetized benefits and results. It also allows for fact-based evaluation of the actionable intelligence project.

Quote to Remember: Did our IT projects deliver their ROI? Did we measure?

Question to Consider: Changing governance models may require cultural change and significant senior support. What needs to occur to position actionable intelligence to follow post-governance?

Notes

1. "Big Data Survey Research Brief," 2013.
2. "Black Budget," *The Washington Post*, September 2013, www.washingtonpost
   .com/wp-srv/special/national/black-budget/.

3. Barton Gellman, Laura Poitras, "British Intelligence Mining Data from Nine U.S. Internet Companies in Broad Secret Program," *The Washington Post*, June 6, 2013, http://articles.washingtonpost.com/2013-06-06/news/39784046_1_prism-nsa-u-s-servers.

4. Veronica Lorraine, "Google Cheat View," *The Sun,* March 6, 2009, www.thesun.co.uk/sol/homepage/news/2350771/Cheating-husband-caught-on-Google-Street-View.html.

5. "Amazing Mind Reader Reveals His 'Gift,'" Safe Internetbanking, Febelfin, 2012.

6. Oracle, "Oracle9i Security Overview," March 2002, http://docs.oracle.com/cd/B10501_01/network.920/a96582/overview.htm.

7. *Encyclopeadia Britannica,* http://global.britannica.com/EBchecked/topic/203373/Federal-Security-Service-FSB.

8. Fabien Soyez, January 27, 2012, owni.eu/2012/01/27/silent-sms-germany-france-surveillance-deveryware/.

Chapter 8

Sustaining Delivery of Actionable Intelligence

Key Points and Questions

- Keep the business sponsors engaged
- Encourage your ambassadors to speak up and share the good news
- Enable fact-based hiring decision for new employees, beyond the interview and the background check
- Implement the Sustainable Training Model I've developed, which has demonstrated success for five years and counting
- Spark cultural change to inspire others to maintain your efforts

In Luo Guanzhong's *Romance of the Three Kingdoms*, Liu Bei, Guan Yu, and Zhang Fei took an oath of fraternity in the Peach Garden (in the modern-day Zhou Zhou, Hebei) to become sworn brothers.

When saying the names Liu Bei, Guan Yu, and Zhang Fei, although the family names are different, we have come together as brothers. From this day forward, we shall join forces for a common purpose: to save the troubled and to aid the endangered. We shall avenge the nation above, and pacify the citizenry below. We seek not to be born on the same day, in the same month, and in the same year. We merely hope to die on the same day, in the same month, and in the same year. May the Gods of Heaven and Earth attest to what is in our hearts. If we should ever do anything to betray our friendship, may heaven and the people of the earth both strike us dead.

The three sworn brothers worked together on a noble purpose: to unite the country of China for the people and instill justice and peace throughout the land. Their effort grew from just the three of them in a garden to running a third of the country. They inspired others to action, built their reputations among the people with quick wins, and brought in an excellent consultant named Zhuge Liang to further enhance their team.

Determine what your purpose is and stick to it.[1] If the book's three main characters worked in a business, Liu Bei, the revolutionary leader of the group, would be the leader of actionable intelligence. He wants to change the entire culture to become fact-based. General Guan Yu would be the business leader, helping to visualize the necessary information and change the processes so that the business can become fact-based. Lastly, Zhang Fei would be the IT leader who will bring the technology and capability to life. The brilliant consultant Zhuge Liang would be a great mentor who guides the team through the politics and challenges it will face.

With a team like this, actionable intelligence efforts can be sustained. In people, process, and technology, it's the technology that builds the actionable intelligence. It's the process that integrates it with the company. But to sustain actionable intelligence you also need people who are hired and trained to work with the actionable intelligence system. Even more so, you need people who trust, people who believe in the new system. That belief is what will truly sustain your efforts. It all starts and ends with the belief that this system you have built from scratch is the solution to data problems.

Leading Intelligence

Belief starts with a leader. Buddha, Moses, Jesus, Muhammad all have one thing in common: They stood firmly for their beliefs and shared with all those who were willing to listen. In his TED talk, Simon Sinek stresses that great leaders stand for something; they believe. Sinek explains it using a concept called "the golden circle:" three circles inside each other that mimic people's thought process. The outer circle, the easiest for people to grasp and use is the "what." To survive, it is extremely useful to have basic skills in recognizing what something is. Everybody can do it. The middle circle is the "how." By determining how the world works we learn about it. This is already less explicit. The inner circle is the "why." The message. It is what links to feelings we have. Gut feelings you could say.

Sinek articulates the what, how, and why model in Figure 8.1 in his TED Talk using Apple as an example.[2]

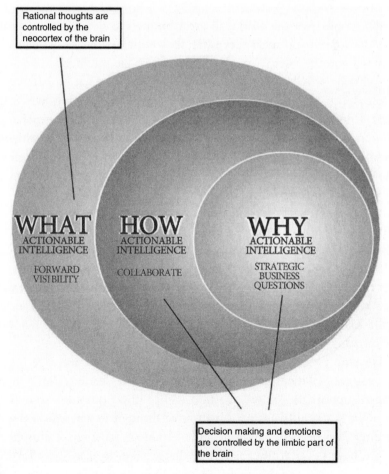

Figure 8.1   What, How, and Why of Actionable Intelligence

If Apple were like everybody else, a marketing message from them might sound like this: "We make great computers [what]. They're beautifully designed, easy to use and user friendly [how]. Want to buy one [why]?" . . . That's how most marketing is done. . . . it's uninspiring.

Here's how Apple actually communicates: "Everything we do, we believe in challenging the status quo; we believe in thinking differently [why]. The way we challenge the status quo is by making our products beautifully designed, simple to use, and user friendly [how]. We just happen to make great computers: want to buy one [what]?"

All prophets of the world, all great business leaders have a message. They do not tell you what they offer, they tell you what they believe in. They tell you the "why." So a leader in actionable intelligence does not sell "what he sells," he focuses on "why he sells it," what he believes in. As a leader in actionable intelligence I believe I am making lives easier (why). I do that by providing answers to the most important strategic questions (how). I happen to deliver that with actionable intelligence capabilities (what). I am not just showing you figures on how well my actionable intelligence tool is doing, I tell you that I believe in what I am saying. I believe I make lives easier.

By now we have determined you are that leader in the effort to deliver actionable intelligence, the one to spark enthusiasm for the project throughout the company. To be honest, I believe in the concept of "leading from every chair," in which everyone in the organization takes ownership of his or her area of responsibility by delivering excellence and striving for continuous improvement. That said, it can and should still be your job to inspire all those leaders and give them a sense of direction.

Develop your own mission and message. When the message is your own, you can sell it best to your employees, business leaders, and sponsors. Vital to support the "why" question is the "how" question, something this book has been painting a picture of through its change in people (Chapter 7), process (Chapter 6), and technology (chapters 2 through 5). But we have never really answered what it takes to lead the effort. Of course all leaders are different and have their own style. That does not mean there are not any universal guidelines for leaders. So here are some pointers for you:

- Focus your energy.
  - What should the company be emphasizing, prioritizing?
  - How much commitment is required for the company to solve the problem?

    Just as a SWOT (strengths, weaknesses, opportunities, threats) Framework makes sure you identify the strategic questions, it's important to communicate with senior leaders regarding their needs. Confirm whether those needs can be addressed and do a force-rank on the priorities. Don't be satisfied with multiple number one priorities, unless they are giving you multiple number one resources. Instead, set expectations clearly so you can succeed and gain the trust we talked about earlier.

- Secure early wins
  - What should you be doing and what should you be avoiding?
  - Does/can the organization bring together the right team to the right place at the right time?
  - How does the team convince the top management to accept the need for change and understand the urgency of the issue?
  - What are the key factors of success and how can they be maintained or improved to ensure their sustainability?

    So you've focused on an issue, the biggest problem typically is getting yourself and the needed resources to focus. That's why you need to have senior management support in the first place. But don't let the means interfere with achieving the end.

Take the risks you think are necessary to deliver while the need to provide the answer is hot. You may need to break down new silos and battle against so-called regulations, but remember you are part of the same company. Engage with that as the foundation and you'll find that even as nervous, turf-protecting senior leaders block access, their junior counterparts who see you are bringing fresh ideas and new capabilities will support you. They will start to believe. At a senior level, ensure your boss is also supporting the effort so if someone does get offended you'll have the upper level support to protect you.

Remember: Focus plus determination plus senior support on a single issue equals a quick win that will lead to a sustainable solution.

Quick Wins to Build Trust

Execution is following through on promises made. James Bond is excellent at influencing good and bad guys/girls to make good on their promises. He is a great salesman. He sells to gain the right support from British Foreign Intelligence Agency Military Intelligence Section 6 (MI6). He sells to infiltrate the bad guys' headquarters. He sells to escape from the bad guys' headquarters and typically closes on other deals on his private yacht in the Caribbean, but we can't mention those here.

Why does "M" trust James Bond so much? Because he always delivers quick wins, and he always beats the bad guys at the end of the day. As a business leader campaigning for change, you need to build intelligence into the process and make it grow from there. Deliver the quick wins like James Bond does.

If you focus on delivering answers to the most critical questions senior management asks, you can build a great reputation. Senior management can't tell customers and Wall Street, "We will give you an answer soon. Our IT department is building a huge data warehouse that will store lots of data. After that we'll create complex algorithms that we won't be able to explain to you, and we still will not know the quality of the data that feeds those algorithms. We won't have eliminated the human gaming that goes on, and we still haven't ironed out how to resolve the unexpected gaps in our financial plans versus our demand plan, but then we'll have the answer."

Naturally, the answer either comes but can't be explained or just never comes. In his book, *The Signal and the Noise*,[4] Nate Silver shares why predictions based solely on data and intelligence are so often wrong. Executives who invest in optimization systems wonder why at first they could show return on investment (ROI), but, soon after the consultants leave, the system starts making bad predictions and business teams return to gaming the system nullifying the initial benefits.

Sustaining any system implementation requires one key ingredient: high adoption stemming from ease of use and real usefulness.

In the Bible, the leaders of the day wanted to eliminate Jesus and his followers because they feared if his teachings spread, it might cause the Roman rulers to crack down on the community. One leader said, "There's no reason to fight against it. If it is not from God then this new religion will fade away just as so many other cults have in the past."

The rest, we know, is history and Christianity still exists 2,000 years later because it is easy to use and provides real usefulness to those who believe.

In contrast, some systems are implemented for reasons of political expediency. For example, one or more executives may have thrown their support behind a big enterprise resource planning and business intelligence system that has not delivered. But the last thing these executives want is someone pointing out a better solution.

It should be clear that leveraging some form of bargaining power cannot guarantee the success of a system, because, in the end, the people without the bargaining power are the ones using it. Even though a leader might have a vested interest in a system, it doesn't mean the system should be maintained. I am a big believer in the phrase, "Don't throw good money after bad." Try to evangelize this phrase, and you'll help your business move faster than your competitors.

In the end, your system will be measured by its success. That's what determines a well-used, sustainable project.

How can we be objective about delivering quick wins? Use a scorecard, or better, use Scorecard and upgrade to Cockpit to make this project visible and mandatory.

Scorecards allow and require that you measure the benefits, or else the scorecard in turn will become based on hunches and guesswork, a result that is completely undesirable in an intelligence project or frankly anywhere at all. So, to measure the quick wins, measure the benefits your projects have achieved so far.

Measuring Successful Business Intelligence Implementations: the Dos

- Do measure the speed of getting to an answer. The online retailer Amazon has the goal of being Earth's most customer-centric company. One of its key metrics is the product load time. Amazon found that even a 100-millisecond increase reduced sales by 1 percent.

Imagine what happens to adoption when every action takes three to five seconds and the expectation of users is milliseconds![3]

- Do measure the number of users regularly accessing your solution. How many people regularly log in at a standard cadence, for example, just before the sales and operations planning meeting.
- Do measure the soft benefits. Has the amount of e-mail needed to find an answer been reduced? Has the number of e-mails containing spreadsheets been reduced? Map the old and new process to show the difference.
- Do measure the hard benefits. How much in revenue or savings have you achieved?

Dashboards and Cockpits

In football, players don't look at a scoreboard all the time; from time to time, they glance at it so that they can make the right plays based on the time left on the clock. At the minimum, scorecards should tell you where you are. Nowadays scorecards—and their close cousins—dashboards—are becoming more and more popular. And now, dashboards can be upgraded to cockpits to be even more interesting and informative to the users.

Dashboard versus Cockpit

- A dashboard shows the status and rate of change of metrics.
- A cockpit allows the business leader to input what-if scenarios on top of the dashboard metrics and see how various levers can impact future results.

The best scorecard should have the capabilities of a cockpit. It allows you to see where you could be and has interrelationships or levers that you can adjust, and it can show you where you might go when you adjust the levers. To achieve this higher level, the business owners need to analyze the relationships between business units, transactions, and nonfinancial to financial performance. This is where you need a very solid business analyst as well as great intelligence analysts to pull the business rules together into a tool/cockpit tool.

Here is an example of a more complete scorecard. First we have the relationships we are establishing between supply chain and finance. This way we can talk across business units easily using the same measurements.

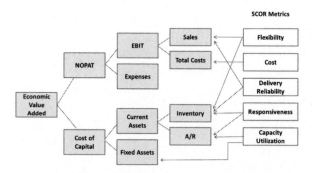

Figure 8.2   Economic Value Added and SCOR Matched Together

The chief financial officer speaks of economic value added (EVA), which is an estimate of a firm's economic profit. It is the value created in excess of the required return of the company's investors (shareholders and debt holders). EVA is the profit earned by the firm less the cost of financing the firm's capital.

The chief supply chain officer speaks in the terms of the supply chain operations reference (SCOR), which is the basis for all supply chain management. The metrics in SCOR provide a solid foundation for measuring performance and identifying priorities; the processes are the common language in your supply chain operations.

Remember collaborating across business functions requires trust, sharing, and a common language. These two models are brought together in Figure 8.2.

Next, Table 8.1 provides a detailed scorecard with performance ratings.

This table shows the directional relationships between SCOR and EVA. Now when it comes to measuring the organization, we set targets and track the performance.

Scorecards should not change (at least not in the short run) but the scores on the board should be changing and improving. Hence, you should make sure that you carry out collaborative business planning to identify the items on the scorecard. You can tally these to show that the subordinate-level data is correct to show the senior executives that the plan is working.

Now, it is time for some final steps: Empower the right people with the right skills and spark in those people a firm belief in what you delivered.

Table 8.1 SCOR Impact on EVA

Metric	Definition	Income Statement			Balance Sheet			
		Sales + Means higher sales	COGS + Means lower COGS	SG&A + Means lower SG&A	Inventories + Means lower inventory	Receivables + Means less receivables	Cash + Means more cash	Payables + Means less payables
Category: People								
% Trained in their discipline at their level	# of staff attending human resources-arranged training for each business unit and level versus year plan.	+	+	+	+	+	+	+
Category: Financial								
Sales revenue to plan YTD	% of sales YTD versus planned sales YTD.	+	+	0	0	0	+	0
Cost of goods YTD %	Cost of goods or services as a % of revenue.	0	+	0	+	0	+	0
Complexity	Count of active products and services. Active means earns revenue and has a cost to serve.	0	+	+	+	0	0	0
% Attainment of forecast	Value of shipments/value of forecast at a selected lag.	+	0	0	+	0	+	0
% Forecast accuracy at product/location level	Forecast accuracy by product or service at a selected lag.	+	0	0	+	0	+	0

Hiring Done Right for Big Data with Big Data

Based on the diagnosis of the business situation, culture, demand for intelligence, and other factors we need to bring in new team members and make sure the current ones are up to par. Are you up for hiring some new talent?

When you are considering expansion, step one is always to clearly determine what is needed in the project. By mapping out what you already have and what skills you need you can make the process a lot simpler and smoother for yourself. After all, you *do* need someone with the particular set of skills you are lacking now.

So assess and inventory your current personnel's skills and how proficient they are in those skills. Then match them up with whatever skills you need to clear the job at hand or for future projects. Is there a gap? Yes? Time to source the skills, either by training or bringing in a new member to the team.

If you decide your team needs someone new, human resources and team leaders need to assess potential team members with good old-fashioned interviewing as well as scanning big data both internally and externally. We need to consider the non-captured data as well as the captured as Nate Silver notes in *The Signal and the Noise*.[4]

The reason for the full review is:

- We are creating a new environment where pace and speed are higher than usual. Whereas IT departments used to be able to deliver intelligence tools in months or even years, now the expectations being set by the best companies are days or at most weeks. The latitude and creativity they need to have now is much higher than they've been used to in the past.
- Knowledge of how to use and develop tools in the toolset is critical to success. If you don't know the tools you can't be a worker. If you can't be a worker, you cannot be a leader. Everyone, top to bottom, should understand the tools of the craft. People unfamiliar with the tools cannot identify opportunities to expand the capabilities. When questions arise as to whether the tool can do this or that, everyone on the project should be able to say yes or no and whether the capabilities are possible in the short, medium, or long term. Knowledge

of capabilities impacts the ability to deliver on time and on budget. More information is better; expectation setting is important.

- As mentioned in Chapter 6, data security is critical, and lost data is tantamount to failure. It must remain secure. The amount of data you'll be exposing to the team is tremendous and needs to be well protected.
- To ensure the potential employee is free of corrupting influences that might cause the person to be forced to hand over sensitive data. Ask about any hidden accounts they may have. As a big data organization, you should establish the ability to comb social media and data within the company.

Do not just interview the candidate; take the person through a two-week training process. Ask him or her to create an actionable intelligence tool and tell a story about it. Your expectation for the tool capability and the story strategy depends on the level of expertise you are hiring. Consider these points on what to look for in the talent:

Higher Level Leaders and Managers
- A higher level person should deliver a great story, be business-driven, results-oriented, and articulate a complete strategy.
- Be great at assessing the business needs.
- Creative in driving ideation sessions to determine the needs.

Technical Resources
- A lower level person should deliver a highly technical tool with all the right capabilities for the job and more, but the story may be basic.
- They should come in ready to deliver. Establish a strong two- to four-week training program so they learn business basics as well as critical technology skills.

In addition, comb through social media information on your latest potential employees on sites like Facebook, LinkedIn, and other social media platforms. Then ask a second time for any hidden accounts. Review these accounts to see who is in the discussions, what activities are discussed, and who they are connected with. Ensure that competitors are not well connected to your candidate.

When going deeper into social media, all companies should have an IT user policy in place that states all communications are owned by the company. Go to the IT department and review the person's files, e-mails, and websites visited to understand their profile. Follow these steps:

1. Run a sentiment analysis and events.
2. Check what attachments were sent to noncompany e-mail addressess. Are there any caustic e-mails that may cause a problem?
3. Even if the individual has sent problematic e-mails, it may not be a reason not to hire him, but rather, be prepared to coach him in a particular way.

Finally, none of this completely replaces good old detective work. Who does your candidate know? What do people think about your candidate?

If there are some red flags that pop up, but you feel the situation can be turned around, you may still want to take a chance on the candidate. Perhaps the manager can coach the new hire on ways to improve.

By doing this exercise, you will strengthen your security and onboarding process, and you will give great feedback to people. Simply by being rigorous in your hiring process you will improve your people factor in people, processes, and technologies. Well done! But don't stop there. After hiring the right workers, you will still need to provide the right training. Proper training encourages proper use and avoids big mistakes. You owe that to the team.

Wait! Don't Hire That Guy Too Fast!

Does anyone else see Eric Snowden's release of classified information to the *Washington Post* and the *Guardian* about government spying as a human resources issue? Whoever let this guy through the vetting process should reevaluate their hiring process.

I sat down with John Ritchie, ex-CIA, current APAC managing director of global security and investigations for a global financial services organization, in his office at Changi Point in Singapore. His view on the change in the intelligence community was point of fact. When he joined the CIA, he trained with a class of 35 people. By the time he left the CIA, the class sizes were up to 500. He felt that the vetting and regular review process might have become overwhelmed, which let Mr. Snowden have too much access.

Eric Snowden and other data leakers speak to the difficulty of scaling the human resources on-boarding process to control quality while at the same time meeting the demands of the business to deliver results. Snowden was a wake-up call.

All your hard work on collecting information can be sent to a competitor with the click of a button. Do your very best to hire and train the right people.

Training

An important part of sustaining the advantage of having actionable intelligence is to keep equipping people with it. If you give people the right tools, but not the instructions to use them, it would have the same effect as giving your CEO a welding torch. It is a very useful tool, but not for the specific function, because the CEO is not trained to use it. For a CEO, a welding torch has the intrinsic value of garbage, whereas to a welder, BI tools would have no intrinsic value.

So far that all sounds logical, however, we hit a bump if we find out the CEO is not trained to wield BI tools. In that case, the CEO cannot capture the benefits and create actionable intelligence, and the BI tool has the intrinsic value of, again, garbage. This is why training is so immensely important, not only for the CEO, but for everyone in the company using BI tools to make more out of their everyday jobs.

There is another potential bump further down the road. As people leave and are replaced, they may have no clue as to what the previous generation did with this so-called actionable intelligence and start from scratch. Slowly, dilution of the knowledge sets in, and regular business practices take over. To help combat this dilution and build an advantage that lasts, I created the sustainable training model for you.

Sustainable Training Model

This model can be used to deliver training to the loyal and enthusiastic team members involved in day-to-day business execution. It's simple, comprehensive, and complete. The people who work in your company are not just employees, they are human beings. They are people with lives outside of work. They may like their jobs, not necessarily love them. They are people who want to succeed but are sometimes let down because of weak processes, poor systems, and incomplete training.

Cliff, Donald, and I have implemented change for years, and we've seen success and failure. Successful implementations have great training, support, and to-the-point documentation.

In 2005, I developed the sustainable training model for our supply base to support the rollout of SAP to more than 3,000 people world-wide. The key principles are:

- People learn in different ways: hearing, writing, doing, testing.
- People need a reason to learn new things.
- Effective post-training documentation is critical.
- "By-your-desk" support must be available.

The four actions needed to implement the Sustainable Training Model are:

1. Ensure the audience recognizes the purpose and need to engage through the executive call to action.
2. Provide training with multiple touch points to build a strong experience foundation.
3. Assess knowledge gained by using certification testing.
4. Follow up and provide easy refreshers to reinforce learnings and solve problems quickly.

We invested in this model for the SAP implementation with great success. So we used it again to deliver actionable intelligence. Business unit leads gave executive calls to action to their teams to use the new tools. We followed up with web conferences, training, FAQs, and town-hall reviews to ensure implementation went smoothly.

Figure 8.3 shows a typical learning curve for a difficult system. An easy-to-use tool set can take less time to learn.

Figure 8.4 shows the types of supporting resources we provided.

Business Cultural Change

Training effectively is not simple. What if the people go to the training meetings, eat the gourmet sandwiches, drink the coffee, go back to their stations, and do what they did all along? Telling people what is required

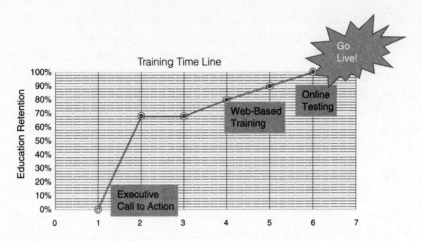

Figure 8.3   Sustainable Training from Start to Go-Live

of them can be easy; getting them to consistently do what is required can be hard. Especially because nobody else in the company is intrinsically motivated to change his or her patterns and habits. So here's another challenge, one of the last obstacles. Cultural change. You must convince people that using actionable intelligence will make their lives easier and more transparent, which is more than just top-down governance change.

The book, *Competing on Analytics*, by Thomas H. Davenport and Jeanne G. Harris,[5] rightly places significant emphasis on the people skills required on the intelligence team. They also mention the need to provide a variety of projects to keep the intelligence team members engaged by constantly learning.

We venture here a bit further by proposing to establish the actionable intelligence team as a shared service. It helps connect business units to support sales and operations, product portfolio management, crisis management, and other enterprise-wide initiatives, which require cross-discipline collaboration.

Actionable intelligence comes to life when areas of the business that don't normally share information begin to do so. There is also a cultural shift required as visibility worries executives.

During business meetings, when a question is asked, in response we sometimes hear, "Let me tell you. . . ." Then we'll hear stories or numbers that someone spouts off the top of his head.

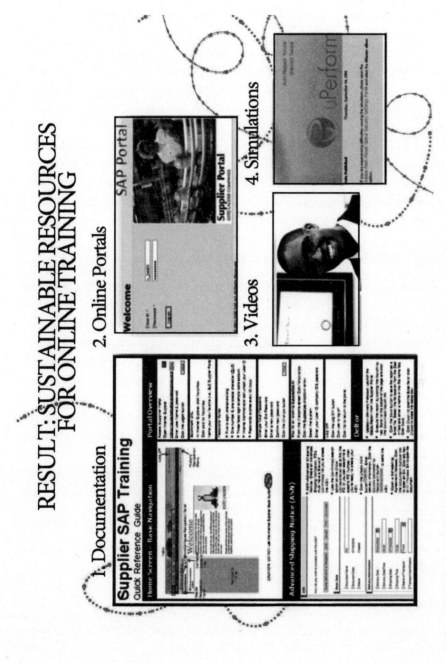

Figure 8.4 Sustainable Training Resources

To become fact-based we need to insist on seeing facts, so the responses to questions should be, "Let me show you." And then she pulls out a mobile device or a computer with the up-to-date facts quickly enough to maintain the momentum of the meeting.

Procter & Gamble provides a wonderful example of this in the article, "P&G Turns Analysis into Action," by Doug Henschen.[6] In the article, Henschen writes that a leader on the business intelligence team said, "Wouldn't it be great if we could give our lead teams all the data they need to make decisions during meetings?"

P&G went ahead and provided a way for remote executives to see the same data visualizations displayed in the meeting room on their laptops or iPads. P&G created, and to this day sustains, a culture of transparency, where information is readily available to all and everyone can and wants to use it.

Use Actionable Intelligence as a Tool, Not a Weapon

Not every company is like P&G; not every company is open to sharing its information. Usually this has one cause: fear. The fear of sharing information comes from the difficulty of accessing it using old business intelligence systems. When there is little sharing, intelligence is seen as the property of the specific business unit and used to make that specific business unit shine. This leads to it being used as a defensive weapon against the rest of the company. This sounds far-fetched, yet it is a real threat.

The efficiencies gained by having facts at our fingertips means more time can be spent looking for opportunities to make the appropriate changes to deliver better results!

Actionable intelligence organizations should have a senior leader in the business who supports the team, but budget should come from each area of the enterprise that is receiving the results.

This exposes the team to business leaders throughout the company, which raises morale and visibility as the successes bloom, resulting in significant benefits throughout the company.

How You Can Enact Cultural Change with Psychology

Organizational culture refers to the behaviors, values, visions, norms, beliefs, working systems, and more that are developed over time by the people

An Example of Using Intelligence as a Weapon

The head of purchasing, John, called me into his office on a rainy day. He looked frustrated. Suppliers had been asking him why the company kept on violating lead times and said it would be difficult to give price breaks if everything needed to be expedited. He asked me for a report that would show whether the planning team launched purchase orders on time or late.

Using older BI systems it took a long time to consolidate a global report as various planning teams used various systems throughout the world. Finally, the report showed the planning teams were placing some purchase orders too late.

The purchasing executive exclaimed, "Ah-ha! So the suppliers are right!"

I called the head of planning and said, "Dan, I just created a report that shows your teams are placing orders late most of the time. Just wanted to let you know."

Dan thought for a moment and said, "Keith, run me a report that shows the purchasing team always places the agreement late."

The report my team created showed that indeed purchasing was placing agreements late.

These two executives were using reports as weapons, because it took time to run business queries. They could go into meetings armed with hard-to-get data and win political battles with a few facts, emotion, and strength of will.

In comparison, after the company visualized the answers to strategic business questions asked by the various business units and made sure there was cross-functional sharing, the finger-pointing stopped and collaboration started.

No one could hide behind a special report, nor could people just say things in meetings; they had to show the facts, giving everyone the same footing.

working in the organization. So you might think you have no power over those elements and, hence, no power over the organizational culture. However, there is a lot you can do to guide behavior, and subsequently guide values, visions, norms, and beliefs of people. Top management can subtly influence the organizational culture with nothing more than a memorandum being handed down.

But rather than settle for top management issuing memos demanding cultural change, you need to transform the organization's psychology and create communities of change to sustain the adoption of the new change. By guiding people's moods in different parts and at different stages of the company and the project you can subtly influence culture.

In order to do that, you need to know what you are going to transform. There are different types of companies with different types of business units working with each other. In the end, it's your job to give every community of practice, whether they are the size of companies, business units, or individuals, the solution to the specific problems they have. It's your time to shine and offer them what they need.

Start with diagnosing your organization's actionable intelligence capabilities by answering the questions posed by Michael Watkins in his book, *The First 90 Days*:[7]

- Where does each part of the organization belong : STaRS (Start-up, Turnaround, Realignment or Sustaining success, see Table 8.2)?
- What are the challenges or opportunities present, and what are the resulting implications?
- Where are the problems coming from?
- What is the cause of the problems?
- Are there any projected solutions, budgets, or time lines for the issue?

Transform the people into successful users, and the adaptation will go more smoothly. This way, you can slowly massage the culture into shape. It's your task to steer different needs toward the common goal. See Table 8.3

You have the power, the control, and the belief. Leverage those to help people with your actionable intelligence. Help them and steer them, and they will become your advocates.

Table 8.2   STaRS

Start-up (unit at the beginning phase)	Turnaround (unit in a downfall)
Realignment (unit continuing steadily)	Sustaining success (unit in an upward trend)

Table 8.3   Transforming Organization Psychology

Stage	Prevailing mood	Transformation
Start-up	Excited confusion: Passionate individuals with a lot of enthusiasm and new ideas flowing freely and in all directions.	• Focus and decide what not to do. • Select the appropriate ideas and projects to develop. • Channel employee energy into the appropriate projects.
Turnarounds	Close to despair: Team members and stakeholders are getting demoralized from one or more setbacks and failures in projects.	• Motivate and encourage teams to keep going and not give up. • Become the light at the end of the tunnel.
Realignments	Denial: Strong individuals who are comfortable with the existing culture and strategy and are resistant to change and realignments.	• Identify the right approach and combination to push the right buttons. • Persevere and deflect all possible resistance and denials to change. • Help the organization to confront the need to reinvent the business.
Sustaining success	Complacent individuals: Employees are beaming with the success that they have achieved and are becoming complacent.	• Create innovation contests to inspire teams to stay hungry, keep thinking. • Challenge individuals to find new growth opportunities to improve themselves organizationally and personally. • Combat complacency and reignite the fighting spirit.

One last tip: Do not forget the message you are steering toward; have it clear at all times when influencing others. Remember to be the bridge for business units to share information and the shining source of information for those same business units to eventually answer the important strategic business questions.

Communication

Are the different departments communicating with each other? Or are they just talking amongst themselves? One important point about creating a culture of sustaining transformation is to make sure that everyone is communicating with each other.

As C. W. Miller wrote in an article, "Actionable Intelligence," in *HR Professional Magazine*,[8] in order for intelligence to be actionable, it needs to be accurate. However, it can be difficult for people to tell the honest truth whenever they are giving opinions and feedback. Likewise, employees may be apprehensive about telling the truth to their fellow employees and, more importantly, their direct supervisors, because they are afraid of the consequences. They may fear that others will become unhappy or offended if they tell the truth, so they make up excuses like: "I don't know them well enough to be giving comments."

In order for an organization to sustain its success, it needs an open culture where people are communicating with each other and telling the truth. Hiding mistakes or telling the CEO that the company is growing when it is falling is not going to help the business. Instead, it may result in more problems over time. Here is an example that illustrates my point.

A friend of mine, Robert Hewardt, was at the time head of product marketing at a software company, Red Hat software. He was trying to establish actionable intelligence to understand the needs of the customers. The strategic question was: When will our customers need our products, so we can be in the bidding process before contracts are awarded?

To gather this data, he needed to pull past contracts and expiration dates, sales quantities, as well as the current sales pipeline and match those with the new capabilities in the updated versions and the planned software release dates from R&D. At first, the effort went smoothly. The head of R&D had no problem sharing the highly confidential release calendar and the product road map. My friend's internal department, of course, let him have the marketing data, and then he had to reach out to IT to gather sales data from the customer relationship management (CRM) system.

The IT person was cordial and understanding. He agreed that indeed, during their own purchasing cycles, the companies that were on top of getting in front of buyers at the right time had a higher chance of success. The meeting went well, and the IT person said he would investigate how to deliver the data for this effort. There were questions such as how the data should be stored, and the timing of updates, and, of course, which IT staff member could be spared to work on the extraction.

The following week the IT person said that the CRM data could not be shared and that no resources would be available for the project. What happened?

Mr. Hewardt found out from his boss, the head of marketing, that the head of sales would not share the CRM data. There was, after all, nothing for him to gain. He knew when the contracts would expire and could ensure his team was chasing down opportunities. It wasn't optimal but it had worked for years. In addition, by having the sales data and pipeline, the marketing team would have seen the true potential sales volume, which may not have matched the lower, but easier to achieve, sales predictions.

To break the silo of sales required that R&D and marketing work together to gain the CEO's support. Although they were all in the same company, they were not yet working in concert. No optimizer can solve this. This requires ongoing teamwork at the sales and operations table.

So in order for the technology to work, you need to align the various department leaders with your goal, and to align the senior management with the goal, you will be supported with the right processes. This is where not only business units need to work in concert, but where you need everything in your project to work in concert with the existing business to achieve and sustain success. Ultimately, that is the main challenge you face. I found success by breaking down the effort into tiny challenges throughout the journey.

Knowledge Lock-In

After establishing a strong foundation of people, processes, and technology you may feel great about having sponsorship, delivering results, and making an impact on the company. If you had been following the advice in earlier chapters about capturing the results from actionable intelligence you may even have saved some actual dollars.

Now it is time to build the capabilities of the organization at large and also bring in knowledge from outside to fill in any gaps you may or may not know exist.

Medium Term
- Have people attend executive education courses like the one I teach.
  - One of the best ways to really lock in knowledge and experience that was gained in the heat of battle is by going back for review in a formal training class. Universities like the National University of Singapore are beginning to offer actionable intelligence courses

tailored for business leaders. These courses go into the details of delivering results leveraging big data and are best taught by practitioners who have actually been in the trenches, fought through the politics, and delivered the results.

- Often-cited case studies certainly provide the class with some foundation, but the personal experiences allow the students to delve deeper into the real details of delivery, which case studies typically lack.
- Another training option for more junior members or business team members who aspire to deliver game-changing results is pursuing a master's degree in business analytics. This offers students the theory, concepts, and methods needed to become world-class decision makers.
- The students graduating from these courses are bringing incredible knowledge back to their organizations. So select candidates or send yourself to formalize your actionable intelligence skillset.
- Bring in external best practices and share internal best practices.
  - After implementing Qlikview and the entire actionable intelligence set of capabilities, I started speaking at conferences about the experience. I've always learned a lot at these conferences both from listening to other presenters as well as networking with professionals who were facing the same challenges. Sharing insights helped me take the implementation much further than I would have without doing so.

    Reevaluate your team and now add data and intelligence to the corporate strategy.

Long Term (Share Externally)
- Participate in building the workforce of tomorrow.
  - Add Qlikview to the classroom. The courses that Keith Carter and I teach are a combination of course material in the area of my expertise and an introduction into the field of business intelligence. This way, I share a new area of business and prepare my students for the future. They are the next generation and can learn a lot from our struggles and successes.
- Present at conferences.
  - When seasoned in the game of implementing actionable intelligence in companies, you might want to think about sharing not just with students but also with practitioners who are currently facing

the same challenges you had. Your guidance at conferences can teach others and help you learn from others as well. I have spoken at the following conferences and found them very engaging and informative:

- FINLAND: 600 Minutes Supply Chain
- SINGAPORE: Healthcare and High Tech Conference by Eye for Transport
- SINGAPORE: Logisym by the Logistics & Supply Chain Management Society
- APAC and EUROPE: Global Supply Chain Management Conference by Terrapinn
- SINGAPORE: Educators Forum by Innovatus
- USA: Gartner Business Intelligence by Gartner
- APAC and EUROPE: Big Data Conference by Terrapinn

- Publish white papers and articles.
  - If talking is not really your thing or if there are no conferences in town, you could also always opt for writing white papers. Usually white papers are published by companies having had firsthand experience with actionable intelligence and its great benefits. You could write about specific aspects and subjects that intrigued you. There's a lot of literature about actionable intelligence but most of it is written by academics and marketing people who haven't actually lived through delivery of the results, the politics, the meetings, the sleepless nights, and the sweat. Join me and contribute with practical experience!

What's Next?

It's in your power to sustain what you have built; it will be your responsibility to sustain your actionable intelligence capabilities. With the Sustainable Training Model you will create your first batch of practitioners that will eventually teach each other. Hiring the right people and formally training them creates great follow-up for many years to come. You have the power to sustain and truly embed actionable intelligence into the organization by changing the organizational culture from within.

Fortunately, some academic institutions are working to fill the gap. In late 2013, I was interviewed by Craig Stires of IDC. In the resulting article based on that interview,[9] he wrote of the University of Singapore's model:

Organizations continue to face a limited pool of resources with effective business analytics skills. Most are facing the need to blend their approach to resolve this between hiring people already holding the right skills, and training existing staff in new disciplines. Singapore is driving towards being an information infrastructure center within the region. It also is home to a number of educational institutions, which are driving to build a stream of resources with the right skills. These programs are critical for laying the right foundations in the people entering the market, particularly in applying technologies and processes to data. Deconstructing business challenges into questions that can be answered with analytics is the art and science of these programs.

Addressing what I am working on specifically, Stires wrote:

The process that Carter teaches is aimed at building a specific mentality of new resources entering the market. He wants people to "dollarize" problems, and make decisions through that lens. Understanding a quantified financial impact to the business of the delay of a particular product launch is what will drive urgency. Statistical relevance may be the underpinning, but attaching opportunities and consequences in strict dollar terms is what will drive action. Carter envisions a near future with waves of students hitting the market, who can build business cases, based on real impacts along the whole value chain.

If business and academic institutions work together, we can improve the teaching and learning programs to graduate students with the skills we need. Indeed, it is unacceptable that after four years of university a student today could still be missing the core skills needed to deliver immediate business results with real-world tools. (The notable exception here is computer science programs.)

The next chapter will make your cultural shift explicit through a mission, vision, and strategy. It will also wrap things up to give you a clear image of what you can achieve.

Summary and Considerations

Point to Ponder: Share the spotlight. Make sure others are shining brightly.

Quote to Remember: "'Walk the floor': See with your own eyes how the new capabilities are being used day to day."

Question to Consider: Have you engaged all the resources in the organization to be purpose-driven about delivering actionable intelligence?

Notes

1. Tom Hulme, Slideshare, July 22, 2013, www.slideshare.net/thulme/ideo-workshop-for-techstars.
2. Simon Sinek, *Start with Why: How Great Leaders Inspire Everyone to Take Action* (New York: Penguin, 2009).
3. Hulme, Slideshare.
4. Nate Silver, *The Signal and the Noise* (New York: Penguin, 2010).
5. Thomas H. Davenport and Jeanne G. Harris, *Competing on Analytics: The New Science of Winning* (Boston: Harvard Business Review Press, 2007).
6. Doug Henschen, "P&G Turns Analysis into Action," *Information Week*, September 14, 2011.
7. Michael Watkins, *The First 90 Days: Critical Success Strategies for New Leaders at All Levels* (Boston: Harvard Business Review Press, 2003).
8. C.W. Miller, "Actionable Intelligence," *HR Professionals Magazine*, http://hrprofessionalsmagazine.com/actionable-intelligence/.
9. Craig Stires, "Buyer Conversation: Addressing the Skills Gap for Actionable Intelligence from National University of Singapore," IDC, 2013.

Chapter 9

Tying It All Together

Key Points and Questions

- Marketing actionable intelligence
- Making a vision, mission, and strategy
- The recipe for success

Clifford Siegel's Journey at Lifetime Brands

Clifford (Cliff) Siegel is executive vice president of the global supply chain at Lifetime Brands, Inc. He leads the sales and operations planning (S&OP) process and enables delivery of thousands of SKUs to customers throughout North America and Europe. Always on the road or busy with family, he was hard to catch up with for this book, but I feel his contribution will help support my contention that actionable intelligence through QlikView is a possibility for any size company in any industry.

I met Cliff through a series of coincidences. I met Linda Levine, saleswoman for Lifetime Brands in early 2009. She arranged a lunch discussion about sales and operations planning with Dan Siegel, executive vice president, Lifetime Brands. During the discussion, Linda and Dan talked so excitedly about their intelligence tools that we simply had to see them. We went back to their office and Cliff kindly took time out of his day to share the tools with us. The tool was amazing, and he is a true evangelist for actionable intelligence and QlikView.

Several years earlier, Lifetime Brands began using SAP R/3 as its back-end business system.

Following standard SAP implementation guidelines, Cliff and his IT team led the implementation of SAP throughout the enterprise. The key benefits of SAP included the powerful capabilities of business intelligence one would expect from a big business system.

SAP was implemented successfully, but the business faced a significant visibility challenge:

- Where were the reports?
- What would they look like?
- Where was the central visibility promised?

Cliff and team worked tirelessly and intensely as scrutiny and frustration increased.

Still the reports they struggled to deliver weren't providing the end-to-end business visibility and needed constant revisions. Cliff and his team looked at examples of SAP reports that cost significant amounts of money but weren't what he expected; for the price, the reporting capabilities were underwhelming. (This was before SAP's HANA, which looks to be impressive.)

Cliff happened to come across a reference call they were doing on behalf of a service provider, and shortly after had a "seeing is believing" event with QlikView—he was duly impressed. Within days, Cliff saw the beginnings of the reports he needed to manage the entire Lifetime business. He purchased the server software and licenses, implemented the QlikView SAP Connector, and placed the server in-house. Then he started to deliver visibility. He realized all this with a small team consisting of himself and several IT people.

Lifetime Brands addressed the critical need for consolidated sales reporting and analysis in its first QlikView application, which tracks sales by specific time periods, months, division, materials, current versus historical, and forecast versus actual—in addition to trend analysis.

He told me, "We are now able to view and analyze sales in every way you could possibly imagine."

Lifetime Brands is using its QlikView sales analysis application to connect data from its budgeting system with data from its customer and sales systems. For example, a single report can access forecast data from the budgeting system and provide a comparison with actual sales from the customer system, providing an integrated view of customer activity. According to Cliff, "Employees at every level are using QlikView every day."

Lifetime Brands has deployed QlikView reports in all functional areas including sales/distribution, finance, and materials management.

Lifetime Brands had a battle plan, a strategy, and acted upon that. That plan allowed the company to build up the key capabilities for actionable intelligence. On top of that, Cliff knew how to sell the idea, the capabilities, and the results to stakeholders.

Clifford Siegel had, at every point, a clear understanding of what he needed to do, how he needed to do it, and where he could get the right people to do it. This is what every business leader needs to be sure of.

Leaders need to aspire and inspire. They need to be able to visualize the big picture and convince the business sponsors, top management, and the rest of the team that they are moving in the right direction. They need the right vision, the right strategy, the right pitch, and the right recipe.

For more information on Lifetime Brands and its success, you can listen to Clifford's story, which is recorded as the Lifetime Brands Qlikview Success Story.[1]

Starting the Right Way

By following Michael Watkin's *First 90 Days*,[2] you can take a fledgling actionable intelligence effort and turn it into a well-supported and sustained effort. Take a look through these steps, and at the end we will walk through an exercise to determine how to tailor your efforts for your current situation.

As Watkins says, companies need to have a structure to implement actionable intelligence. So here is a summarized seven-step strategy to start with:

Step 1. Build a reputation for delivery of fast actionable intelligence. Let people know what you are doing.

Step 2. Accelerate learning. Learn actionable intelligence quickly. Learn as much as you can about the people, process, and systems strategy.

Step 3. Match your sustaining strategy to the culture and business situation.

Step 4. Negotiate success. Be clear that actionable intelligence alone doesn't bring success; people actually have to take action. It's a joint success.

Step 5. Build your team. Evaluate your needs and put together your team from both the people you've inherited and people you will hire to form a complete small team and then deliver improvements and scale as necessary.

Step 6. Create coalitions. Bring together IT and business leaders and make sure they all get credit and are all incentivized to support your effort.

Step 7. Motivate everyone. Make sure that you instill a sense of urgency within everyone who's engaged. And the urgency is not just to see results but also for them to increase their skills, knowledge, and capabilities.

As mentioned throughout this book, earn credibility fast by delivering results immediately.

Finding the Right Pitch

The marketing of actionable intelligence is as important as the delivery. Here we wrap up the capabilities we've been talking about into the communications tools used by senior management: a catchy phrase, a mission statement, a strategy, and a call to action.

First, the wording is important. I called the capabilities actionable intelligence and our team supply chain intelligence because when we think of business intelligence we immediately think of IT delivering reports.

Actually, we should have the feeling of confident, fact-based business decisions. Business intelligence is too IT focused, and the landscape is littered with business intelligence failures.

How about analytics? Getting closer, but the word analytics gives the impression of a scientist, sitting for days, months, or years analyzing while managers sit paralyzed without information . . . indefinitely.

Tell people that you are in intelligence. Their minds immediately jump to James Bond's line of work. The word intelligence elicits the feeling of speed, crispness, focus, even danger, and rightly so; every day we make decisions impacting careers, lives, and safety.

Adding a descriptor to the word intelligence is important to shape the impression. Corporate intelligence, competitive intelligence, market intelligence, supply chain intelligence—these are phrases that indicate the work we do provides businesses with the actionable intelligence needed to make fact-based decisions right now.

Be bold, do not just settle for the phrase of the day. Create one that matches the capabilities you provide!

Developing a Mission and Strategy for Intelligence Capabilities

You will not turn around the entire company with a phrase. So why not make your change explicit with your plan to win! By providing your team with a mission, vision, and strategy you will create strong morale. Now, how should we go about doing that?

Gary Hamel, in a *Harvard Business Review* article,[3] suggests recognizing three kinds of companies. What he dubbed the "Industry Lords" are current market leaders and usually large conglomerates. Then come the "Industry Peasants," whose main goal is to become the future Industry Lords. And last, though especially not least, are the "Revolutionaries" or the "Rule Changers." This is the group in which strategy takes flight, according to Hamel.

Hamel says the focus on incremental improvements can potentially be deadly, when competition is focused on reinventing the wheel and revolutionizing the way customers see the product. The issue is mainly a psychological one. Challenging resident beliefs might invoke change, for better or worse. Inherently this brings about some form of stress, risk, and uncertainty. Why rock the boat when the company can simply remain a profitable, leading organization in its market. The problem with this is, whereas people inherently dislike change, companies welcome all help to beat competition by changing everything in the game, up to the game itself. This revolutionizing is worthy of the name "strategy," according to Hamel; everything else is called tactics.

The following four steps formulate a strategy to create actionable intelligence.

Step 1: Let People Provide Ideas

Companies are led by people with ideas, and can, in turn, encourage or discourage the creative process. To quote Leonardo DiCaprio from the movie *Inception*: "An idea is like a virus: resilient, highly contagious. The smallest seed of an idea can grow. It can grow to define or destroy you."

This quote captures the pure essence of ideas, the starting point of strategy creation. The right ones might be strong enough to define you, the wrong ones can destroy your worth. However, having people with great ideas might not be enough to revolutionize a company. Here is where further steps come into play.

Step 2: Ensure Collaboration between the Business and IT

Ron Price[4] accurately identifies these steps, starting with the notion that none of us, however brilliant the idea may seem, should put all our eggs in one basket. People always reflect on their own ideas more positively than others do. Price says that reaching instant consensus does not automatically signal a good thing going.

After critical deliberation and the creation of alternatives to choose from, it might be sensible to ask stakeholders in the future strategy for buy-in through their perceptions of the new (radical) strategy. There might be some resistance. Perhaps even a lot of resistance to what you are about to deploy. Giving up now doesn't get you anywhere. Instead, challenging resistance helps deliver revolutionary change. Challenging your own beliefs also provides fresh, new direction. Challenging your own beliefs transcends a personal level. Business functions should hold ideation sessions with other functions, not just themselves. In particular, they should brainstorm with IT to reach the best technology-challenging ideas of today for the company of tomorrow.

Step 3: Define How to Measure Success

One of the most powerful tools in business is benchmarking. In each meeting, look at industry best practices. Set the goals of the desired strategy and try to avoid using past goals, which may not drive the right behavior to deliver the new strategy.

Benchmarking delivers the sense of urgency and accountability people need to drive strategy and new ideas through the process of being incorporated and executed properly. Because what good would ideas be, if they always stay ideas?

Step 4: Engage the Organization Top to Bottom and, as Usual, Work Iteratively

Keep these points in mind:

- Strategy creation is an iterative process, which sometimes goes faster than you would want. New revolutionary waves of strategy creation can start even before the last wave has subsided.
- Great ideas do not always come from key executives. Anyone can be an advocate of change, thus everyone needs a platform to share their ideas. In universities, Google has always been considered an exemplary company, closely abiding by this rule.

Strategy creation is the process of daring to challenge all you believe in for the sake of better results. There will be bumps in the road to positive, lasting, and radical change, though many good ideas up until this day have been a major success story.

So let us take a look at an example so that you can have a clearer idea of what I am trying to convey. Use these as guides, but make your own. The buy-in and understanding of the people you work with is more important than the words!

A Sample Mission Statement of Delivering Actionable Intelligence Capabilities

Deliver actionable intelligence at the speed our business needs to make fact-based decisions and attain our business goals.

A Possible Actionable Intelligence and Data Management Strategy

1. Ensure the organization has timely, accurate data needed to run the business and deliver improvements with excellence.
   - Create and maintain a dedicated business-led organization to support the data management and reporting processes. Align the organization with IT to drive results.
   - Create and maintain a data management strategy to clarify data ownership, standardize the business language, and promote integration across all business processes.
2. Leverage actionable intelligence for fast, accessible, and relevant facts.
   - Provide facts to set priorities, select tactics, execute with excellence, and monitor success.
   - Promote agility by accelerating information flow.
3. Enable the organization with capabilities for fact-based insights, decisions, and actions.
   - Leverage information capabilities to support accuracy, efficiency, and adoption of modernized processes, drive out non-value-added costs, and help better understand business needs and performance results.
   - Build the capabilities, and take action on intelligence.
   - Stay focused on the biggest opportunities with governance.

Now try to formulate your own mission statement and strategy.

TIE: The Intelligent Enterprise at STATS ChipPAC with Elizabeth Lim

Let us take a look at STATS ChipPAC, a turnkey semiconductor packaging, design, bump, probe, assembly, test, and distribution solutions service provider based in Singapore. With manufacturing plants across Asia, the company has been recognized for excellence in delivering technology innovation, manufacturing excellence, and cost competitiveness.

I met Elizabeth Lim at the Qlikview Business Discovery World Tour. She was a fellow presenter whose presentation caught my interest. They had gone through the same journey as I had but with Information Technology (IT) leading the effort instead of the business. Important to note is that Elizabeth was a director at this time.

I met her at her office in Ang Mo Kio, Singapore, nestled in an industrial park nicely landscaped with palm trees and overlooking a grassy field with a view of the city beyond. It was a serene place to discuss a business intelligence strategy.

When the company started off on its business intelligence journey, it was driven by the need for three things:

1. A decision support system that would help with executing projects, expanding the strategic global footprint, and improving process and quality controls.
2. Single and integrated information about all SKUs by category, type, site, and more.
3. Faster and effective information delivered to decision makers and leaders across all sites to support supply chain strategizing, material cost management, and competitive pricing.

With that, the company started The Intelligent Enterprise (TIE) that was designed to help the company be equipped with the actionable intelligence to maximize the quality of revenue, capacity, and opportunities, and minimize costs.

The objectives?

- Enable speed and agility to business questions
- Establish data quality to support business questions
- Integrate data for holistic analysis
- Establish information security
- Establish data governance
- Reskill and retool knowledge workers

They focused on three main areas:

1. Demand management information integration for insights on historical revenue versus forward forecasts to maximize capacity allocations
2. Operational capacity utilization and cost minimization
3. Test as part of turnkey

STATS ChipPAC's actionable intelligence effort was successful because of five factors:

1. The CEO had the vision and provided the strategic directives for TIE.
2. The COO and CIO on the TIE Steering Committee acted as the business sponsors and spent time reviewing and dealing with the situation.
3. There are user champions or subject matter experts who advise on where to get the data from, ensure the quality and accuracy of the information, and determine how to best use it.
4. A data governance team that includes data owners and is directed by the corporate finance team.
5. IT-initiated and business-engaged. They are maturing to the point where the business is taking ownership, and that is when they will start to see real dollars as a result of their implementation.

In addition, the company measured report usage and conducted business scenario training as well as mass trainings through self-service videos to equip its people with the right skills. Ms. Lim's IT department also shared project key performance indicators (KPIs) to ensure cooperation and integrated the entire company from data to functions, people and similar objectives. Qlikview provided the information automation while export to Excel from Qlikview reports are practical for large tables and what-if analysis. Two major challenges were the momentum required to overcome user reluctance to start using the system and the response time degradation as more users got on board.

After setting up the critical mass of data and the technical infrastructure, STATS ChipPAC leveraged Qlikview to deliver dashboards that showed employees the level of performance, for example, loss utilizations; how customers were affected; the specific products involved; and the source of the issue. This allowed them to zoom in and take action quickly and achieve their objectives.

A key point that you should be taking note of is that even though the project was IT initiated, the business was engaged during the process.

The results weren't just tangible for the company. I met with Elizabeth Lim several months after implementation and she had been promoted to chief information officer (CIO). It's wonderful to see a company support the growth of a person who leads game-changing results.

Now STATS ChipPAC has matured as a company to the point where it needs the business users to deliver insights from the intelligence tools. The business users and leaders in the best companies embed intelligence analysis and storytelling into their regular business reviews. With rapid intelligence, companies can be more nimble, but only when they also update their processes such as moving from annual to monthly business reviews or establishing weekly cadences for collaborative business planning.

Business–Led versus IT–Led

The business needs to take charge of the process of leveraging big data and actionable intelligence because it is the one in charge of delivering results, not IT.

Projects can be started by anyone in the company, be it the business executive who wants to have his problems solved or the smart IT guy with an idea that can help the company. Regardless of in which department the project is started, the ultimate goal is to have the business take accountability for delivering results with the new capabilities. Figure 9.1 should be used to select which business unit should be accountable.

So why can it not be IT? Because IT is only a support department, which typically is not responsible for delivering results. IT's KPIs are necessarily different from those of the business. Sometimes, they are in conflict with each other. Between the IT team in charge of the success of the IT

Figure 9.1 Shared Services Ownership Should Be Based with an Innovative Leader Who Understands the Greatest Needs

network upgrading project and the manufacturing officer in charge of the production of 10,000 SKUs, their needs, challenges, and targets are different.

The IT team may be able to infer from the stories they hear what the problems are. However, the nuances of how an intelligence tool will be used in the various processes are only known by the business and sometimes those employees do not even know until they try it out.

Business units need to take charge and learn how to take ownership of not only the results but also the journey. They need to be inculcated with the use of actionable intelligence to make the right decisions that IT cannot make.

If IT continues to lead the project:

- The business will never fully appreciate actionable intelligence, and it will slowly fade away as a project.
- The culture of being fact-based won't be instilled.
- The change in business processes won't be sustained.
- The main beneficiary of these capabilities won't appreciate owning the responsibility.

The next best thing is for IT to exchange staff into the business and bring some business people into IT. This way, both organizations benefit from cross-integration.

The biggest risk is not completely syncing the capabilities with the business needs. That will lead to low adoption, and during an economic downturn the business will ask to make cuts without fully understanding the impact.

The Recipe to Greatness

Whether you are leading, supporting, or part of delivering actionable intelligence at your firm my advice is this: Do not get caught up with words like big data or the dollar signs accompanying big systems. Stay focused on delivering answers to the strategic business questions that are most important but are hard to answer without a full picture.

Engage the business and make them strong partners in design, usage, and benefits achieved. Break the habit of gut instinct and replace it with fact-based decision making that relies on actionable intelligence.

Engage IT and break the mold of the software development life cycle. Break down the silos by encouraging IT staff to rotate into the business and share responsibility for business results.

Finally, deliver actionable intelligence, capture the monetized benefits, and improve the business.

And one more thing. What follows is a recipe of ingredients proven to deliver actionable intelligence:

- **One spoonful of purpose-driven passion**
  - What drives you? Select your own personal mission, and remember that people adopt products and services that help them achieve their dreams and bring them closer to achieving their aspirations.
  - Have the drive to embark on delivering actionable intelligence to the company as well as the perseverance to deliver the intended results.
- **One or two strategic business questions to focus on**
  - The business leaders need to be part of the project. Don't start without a specific question. Don't start if the vision of using actionable intelligence hasn't been made clear.
  - Don't start with too many projects. You will be better off under-promising and overdelivering than the other way around.
- **Organization leaders who know they can do better**
  - Gain support at the C-level and the support of several of those executives' direct reports in order to break down silos. When leaders are providing the strategic directives to the project, it lays the foundation for change management and facilitates the sharing of data across business silos.
- **One or more senior leaders/business sponsors** to support the effort by removing obstacles and enabling results
  - The senior leader will become your background support so that when business units are not willing to share or IT security is concerned with regulatory policies, he or she will provide you with some of the information that you need or simply change the policies in your favor.
  - This leader should be a seasoned executive, skilled in maneuvering around politics, and regarded as an influencer and a mentor.
  - *They will* spend time reviewing and utilizing the answers to strategic business questions.

- **One business-led approach** to support the culture and mindset change required when new technologies are implemented and strategic business questions are being answered
  - Why business-led over IT-led? The business already has ownership of the results. Thus, these employees need to be educated to also take ownership of the journey. They cannot survive by always executing the old way. They need to be trained to use actionable intelligence to make decisions. While IT can guide the business—even serving as the pilot in the beginning—it is more like the driving instructor teaching a student to drive. At the right point, the student takes the wheel of the car as a business leader takes the wheel of the business unit.
  - Implement one mission, one team methodology and galvanize around a call to action; team name; or some image, symbol, or flag; and make sure to always align to the corporate strategy. This ensures that you are seen as part of the company's success.
- **One budgeting process** that supports actionable intelligence
  - Businesses need to have a post-governance model to support quick achievement of results in iterative, reviewable increments while avoiding the slow paperwork of standard governance models.
  - Budget line items include core functions like on going support, licensing, and testing; new capabilities like future enhancement; new tools and insights captured; transformation governance; master data management; training, development, and travel and expense for onsite change management.
- **One or more advisors** who know where the relevant data resides
  - They know where the data is throughout the systems, what it is called, who to ask to get the data security permission, and how often it is refreshed.
- **One data acquisition team** to manage the data needed to answer the question. The team also provides a trusted, verified source of the truth
  - Every great intelligence organization has a strong acquisition team, whether it is the U.S. National Security Agency or the Singapore Internal Security Department, they have a mandate to aggressively acquire data.
  - Corporations need to enable the same capability in the actionable intelligence team.

- **One data dictionary** to act as a cross-reference between business terms and related data fields
  - Have the same names and terms for all the data fields so that the different departments are able to speak the same language and communicate with one another better.
- **One central repository**, dead simple to use, easy to control, edit, update, and cheap
  - In order to ensure that information can be easily accessed, organizations should have a central repository to store all the data in one location. No more phone calls, e-mails, and waiting for days to go through different people in order to get the information.
  - Be careful not to create more siloed functions in the process of acquiring the central repository.
- **One visualization team** responsible to deliver rapid, iterative answers in a business discovery tool
  - What is more important than acquiring information is understanding the information. When complex and complicated pieces of information are delivered to decision makers, the lack of time and understanding of the data may encourage them to revert to using gut and intuition. Hence, it is important for companies to have a business discovery tool that can help to visualize the information into simple-to-understand business insights and facts and do it quickly and effectively to support the decision-making process.
- **One business discovery software tool** that is easy to install and able to start small and scale big. Today, that tool is QlikView.
  - Businesses need to be able to discover the information within their four walls and outside. Relying on Microsoft Excel spreadsheets to handle the data is no longer sufficient . Business needs to have a business discovery tool that will enable it to adopt easily and develop to grow greater.
- **One or more forward-looking intelligence tools** made by the team mentioned previously to provide answers to the strategic questions asked by the sponsor
  - Every company is different, and every department or team requires a different intelligence tool to cater to its needs and answer its strategic questions. When tools are self-developed, they tend to be more user-friendly and better suited to the team's needs, because

the team developing them knows that they are the ones using the tools. Make better proactive decisions with the tools; do not just perform reactive fire-fighting.

- **One adoption and insights person** who engages business people in value realization
  - One of the most important individuals on the team who ensures the delivery of results but is commonly deprioritized.
- **One data management team** acting as air-traffic control to orchestrate success
  - Go to each person's desk and monitor the use of actionable intelligence tools to see how they use them and help them monetize the use.

Remember to start small, and demonstrate fast success. With the right foundation, you will achieve significant benefits.

The result of the recipe:

- **Monetized business improvements** making the whole team proud.
- **Passionate business ambassadors** who share the results with their colleagues.
- A joyful you, who has joined us on the purpose-driven journey to improve the lives of others by giving them the answers they need to make better decisions faster and easier.

Table 9.1 can be used to assess where you are. Please feel free to fill this in online at: www.keithbcarter.com so you can share your situation, challenges, or successes with me.

Table 9.1 Checklist of Capabilities

Recipe Item	Estee Lauder	STATs ChipPac	Lifetime Brands	Your Company
Type of company	Luxury FMCG	IT Semiconductor	Consumer Products Mfg.	
Purpose-driven passion	✓	✓	✓	
Business questions to focus on	✓	✓	✓	
Company leader who believes they can do better	✓	✓	✓	

Table 9.1 (*Continued*)

Recipe Item	Estee Lauder	STATs ChipPac	Lifetime Brands	Your Company
Senior manager who can clear obstacles	✓	✓	✓	
Business sponsor	✓	✓	✓	
Business-led	✓	IT-led, business enabled	Shared leadership	
Advisors to support with data acquisition	✓	✓	✓	
Data acquisition team	✓	✓	✓	
Data dictionary	✓	✓	✓	
Central repository	✓	✓	✓	
Visualization team	✓	✓	✓	
Business discovery tool	✓	✓	✓	
Forward-looking intelligence tool	✓	✓	✓	
Adoption and insights in charge	✓	✓		
Data management team	Successful	Successful	Successful	

Summary and Considerations

Point to Ponder: Use benchmarking to know what great looks like.

Quote to Remember: "The tipping point is that magic moment when an idea, trend, or social behavior crosses a threshold, tips, and spreads like wildfire." —Malcolm Gladwell

Question to Consider: What is your strategy for actionable intelligence?

Here's a mini quiz for you:

Who is accountable for the data strategy?

    a. C-level executives

    b. Line-of business executives/VPs

    c. IT executives

Answer available at www.keithbcarter.com.

Notes

1. QlikView, "Lifetime Brands Unlocks Data in SAP and Other Systems for Seamless Analysis with QlikView," http://www.qlik.com/us/explore/customers/customer-listing/l/lifetime-brands.
2. Michael Watkins, *The First 90 Days: Critical Success Strategies for New Leaders at All Levels* (Boston: Harvard Business Review Press, 2003).
3. Gary Hamel, "Strategy as Revolution," *Harvard Business Review*, 1996.
4. Ron Price, "The Four Ps of Strategy Creation," 2009, http://callcenterinfo.tmcnet.com/analysis/articles/55147-four-ps-strategy-creation.htm.

Chapter 10

Next Frontiers

Key Points and Questions

- With the advent of digitized information, we now have the capability to integrate, analyze, and exploit both structured and unstructured data. Our ability to understand and learn from data has been transformed, enabling us to move from the era of information to the era of insight.
- What kind of information would enable leaders in any industry to make better decisions? Whether health care, education, transportation, manufacturing, banking, or retail, there are constant basic questions: "What is the current situation?" and "What should we do next with limited resources?"
- "The rise of human-computer cooperation in solving big problems has never been about simply finding the right algorithm but rather finding the right interface between the data-crunching capability of machines and human ingenuity."[1]
- The future and possibilities with big data and actionable intelligence are endless.

How do you feel about a cashless society? One where everyone has a global identification number based on their DNA. No need to carry wallets filled with credit cards, and various countries' currency. Just walk up to a retailer and transact business or even look at a particular item with Google Glass and subtly click with your eye movement to make the purchase.

In 1995, I was on a bus with my fellow Andersen Consulting start-group members and, as usual, I wanted to take a poll. Would they enjoy a cashless society? Everyone said "yes" emphatically! When I asked why, they cited convenience and safety as the key reasons. Not surprisingly, privacy was not top of mind for these 20-something-year olds . . . and 20 years later, it still really isn't so much as demonstrated by social media's up take.

Harnessing big data about people at a DNA level would allow our products and services sector to use actionable intelligence at every turn. The ultimate unique identifier would make travel easy. Pickpockets would become an anachronism, and ATM would fade away.

Insurance companies, banks, and hospitals would be at the ready to react to the needs of people as they foresee opportunities. The utopia of human services would no longer be a dream but a very real reality.

More than 2,000 years ago, John, a disciple of Jesus, wrote in Revelations that a time would come when all buying and selling would require a mark on the hand or forehead. This globally unique number would be used in all transactions.

Even today it is difficult to imagine the speed and connectivity of a global transaction system for all countries and a single currency. But it is much easier to demonstrate with the global banking system, ease of using ATMs, or swiping a credit card.

All this leads to capabilities we should provide to achieve actionable intelligence.

Intelligence can no longer just be restricted to specialists; it has to be accessible for everyone.

— Keith Carter

Here are some key deliverables of actionable intelligence when all the previously mentioned activities are put in place:

- Actionable intelligence executed rapidly at all levels in organizations. Sitting on top of big data and stacks of so-called business intelligence reports with the business leading the way to deliver game-changing insights.

- The organization will receive answers to strategic business questions in hours instead of days. Minutes to refresh tools not hours or weeks.
- Data should be refreshed every second and every moment.
- Data needs to be validated at all times *before it is published for decision making*, and if it is wrong, alerts need to be communicated and problems resolved.
- Corporate leadership will be receiving daily briefs similar to the senior leadership brief that senior government leaders receive daily from their intelligence organization. The intelligence would be in the right format, security, and level of detail for the receiver whether it's sent to a department/division/function/global head. Both the internal and external aspects of their business are viewed and people on their teams follow playbooks to take actions.
- Answers will be as accessible as walking down the hall, like the hospital information system. Everyone is able to answer questions with "let me show you" facts by immediately using a secure mobile device or conveniently located computer.
- Everyone has a big data device that visualizes the situation at any time and matches a dynamically updating set of actions to take based on the situation with a feedback loop to further improve the proposed actions.

"Actionable intelligence is not a one-way street. In the future, once you make a decision you should be able to make a change directly from the intelligence system into the transactional system," added Clifford Siegel, senior VP, Lifetime Brands.

Following are some ideas that show the practical applications of actionable intelligence outside a business context, because actionable intelligence can affect all of us.

A Healthier Lifestyle with Actionable Intelligence

In the movie, *The Island*, human clones conduct simple medical tests like blood tests every morning to track their overall health. The information is passed on to the cafeteria ladies who will be empowered with the data to restrict their diets, like banning bacon if the sodium levels are too high.

In hospitals today, doctors will order diet restrictions for certain patients with certain medical conditions. This ensures that patients are eating right during their stay. But what happens about everyone else outside the hospital?

If you are a patient with high cholesterol, high blood pressure, and high blood sugar who loves to eat, it can be hard to resist the aromatic *char kway teo*. A In addition, since there is no one monitoring you, you might just join the queue even though the doctors said that it is unhealthy for you. What if there is a form of technology available to guide you with those restrictions? What if the moment you join the queue, a warning sign appears on your Google Glass that directs you toward the healthier vegetarian food stall or the salad bar?

Sounds restricting, but as little kids we sometimes needed guidance to eat our veggies. Do we really think that as adults we have full freedom to ruin our health or cause others the pain of seeing us make bad life choices?

The Street-Smart Cabbies

When I was in New York, it was always very difficult to flag a cab. Some of the taxis would drive by even though they had no passengers—a common situation in almost every country in the world. I once asked a taxi driver if drivers sometimes ignored would-be passengers. He told me about the time when a teenager hired his cab to go back to his university campus. Upon arriving, the student suddenly exited the cab and disappeared into the mass of students without paying.

As humans, we will automatically fill in the details of the story based on our experience and expectations. Although I didn't mention gender, you will think it was a boy, although I didn't mention race, your brain will pick one automatically. Cabbies do the same thing. After all, there is too much information for us to treat everyone as unique individuals—we were made to generalize to survive a challenging environment.

Cabbies in New York could have a tool that tracks who gets into their cab, similar to the devices that track who walks into the mall. This device would pick up the unique identification of the cell phone and store it as well the reputation of the passenger. No need to capture exact details like name or such; although, if a fare skipper did try to get away, the police could be handed the information along with the pictures (cabs in New York always take photos on entrance and exit), then they could easily track and apprehend the perpetrator.

It is inevitable that cabbies will be picky about the customers they pick up. There is a difference between the stingy person who doesn't tip and the regular taxi passenger who gives a $5 tip every time. There is a difference between the good citizen with good moral values and the teenager who dashes out without paying the fee. There is also a difference between the timely individual who reserves a cab and is always ready to be picked up and the customer who regularly is late or, worse, cancels his reservation frequently.

So what happens if we introduce big data and actionable intelligence for cabbies? With a big-data-enabled device, cabbies could be driving down the street looking for fares, and seeing people overlaid with cab usage data. Imagine on both sides of the street people outlined in green (1 and 3 in Figure 10.1) if they are "safe" based on past actions, red (4 in Figure 10.1) if they have done cabbies some wrong in the past, and gold (2 and 5 in Figure 10.1) if they are great tippers or regular customers.

In New York, the world renowned actor Danny Glover complained to the Taxi and Limousine Commission (TLC) because he got frustrated with cabs simply driving past him because of his race and the location he wanted to go to in the city.[2] Privacy advocates will instantly complain about too much information being shared with strangers, but the typical

Potential Customers / Risks Facial Recognition System
1. Male 60-70 yrs, OK customer
2. Male 60-70 yrs, unknown
3. Female 50-60 yrs, OK customer
4. Male 50-60 yrs, BAD skipped fare
5. Female 30-40 yrs, unknown
6. Unidentified

Figure 10.1 Being Identified for Opportunities or Threats by Cabbies
PHOTO CREDIT: Gary McCabe, November 2010, Flickr.com Creative Commons License.

privacy advocate is not the demographic who gets ignored by cabbies. The benefits of treating good customers well and being protected from bad customers may outweigh privacy concerns.

This again is big data, but it doesn't require prediction. In fact, prediction is where we can go wrong by not having a complete model. In fact, a predictive model might increase discrimination because of several key flaws.

- The model tends to track higher levels of demographic information when incidents are reported. The first incident where the young person ran into the fancy university might not have been reported by the cabbie. Whereas an incident in another neighborhood could be reported, so we are at the mercy of the thoroughness of incident reporting.
- There could be bias in the reporting, which may list the demographic information incorrectly.
- Past performance is not an indicator of the future. The demographic or location that has a disproportionate number of incidents reported can change or may have good people mixed in, which is most often the case. The data scientist who simply monitors data would misdiagnose the model and perpetuate discrimination.

Personally, I am a big tipper of cabbies in New York, because I do want to change their impression of a demographic that I am associated with, so I take this personally and appreciate Danny Glover's attempts to improve the New York TLC.

The Amplified Customer Experience

The profusion of smartphones and tablets in recent years has changed the retail landscape, contributing to an ongoing shift in the balance of power firmly toward the hands of the customer. Armed with a relatively inexpensive mobile device, shoppers have instant access to facts, opinions, and reviews and can compare prices on just about anything they might be interested in buying—be it from their local corner store or an online retailer operating out of giant warehouses on the other side of the world.

The combination of mobile device and data plan effectively gives customers a "big data license," bringing ready access to a wealth of product and retail information.

One U.S. survey, for example, found that 59 percent of consumers said they regularly use their smartphones while shopping in retail stores to compare prices for the same or similar products.

But of course it is not only prices that can influence purchase choices. Having a big data license also allows customers access to a broad swathe of other information, including:

- Social media sentiments about the product in question
- Rumors of upcoming versions
- Friends' views on the items
- Recent celebrity endorsements
- How a specific store's sales staff treats people
- Pros and cons of competitor or alternative products

With this depth of information at their fingertips, customers are now in a stronger position to know more about specific products than the salespeople in the store.

Selling Better

In the space of just a few years then, and with relatively little conscious effort, customers have changed their processes and technology, leveraging big data to enable them to make the ultimate purchase decision: "Do I buy this here and now?"

With so much data-driven power in the hands of customers, the obvious question then is where does this leave the salesperson?

Do they have the right information to sell their products to the customers better? And, if they do not, how do they go about getting it?

Given the volume and value of customer information offered by big data, the salesperson should also know all the details about customers as they walk through the door.

Instead of judging the customer's outward appearance, the salesclerk can know:

- What is the value of the customer and her purchasing power?
- Is he a repeat customer at the store or other outlets? If so, what does he normally like?

- Who are your customers' friends and influencers? What products are their friends interested in? What have they bought previously?
- What did they tweet, post on Facebook or Instagram before, during, or after shopping at your store?
- Do they normally shop at a competitor, and is this a possible conversion opportunity?
- What country does she come from, and what is her preferred language?

Let us take a couple of examples that offer important lessons for retailers in terms of the way they connect with their customers.

At one end we have traditional owner-operated retailers, such as the long-running wet-market stalls across Singapore. In my own neighborhood, the Chan family-owned fresh chicken stall has served customers for 50-plus years. They've developed a comfortable familiarity with their customers and are able to tailor their sales to specific customers.

On the other extreme, we have the online mega-retailers such as Amazon.com or Singapore's Q0010.sg, that monitor and utilize customer data very carefully, making recommendations to the customer when they return or sending targeted, personalized e-mails to bring them back for more.

In both examples, customization has led to increased sales and service levels.

The challenge for a chain operation is that the salesperson is different at each store. That raises the question, can—and should—customer information be shared to provide personalized service?

Serve Me Better . . . But Don't Intrude on My Private Life

Of course, retailers with customer data need to balance building a great image with the delivery of personalized service against the risk of being seen as invasive.

Some of us are willing to spend a little extra time going to the cosmetics artist we trust, a few extra dollars to go back to that particular restaurant, or travel that extra mile to that nice coffee shop that is kind of on the way home.

But there are days when your favorite make-up artist isn't in or the familiar coffee barista has a day off, or times when you are just at a different outlet. You lose all the usual benefits, the warm welcome, and most importantly, the connection and status of a regular customer.

What if this personalized human touch could be applied to all retail stores across all of one chain's outlets and maybe even across the world?

When the service person was known to us, even a friend, we can be certain of the personal touch. But what about when it is someone we have never met before?

Imagine walking into the Starbucks on the other side of town. The store assistant is able to welcome you back with a warm smile and address you by name, even though you have never set foot in the store before. And, even before you show them your Starbucks card or credit card or tell them your order, the assistant asks whether you would like your usual coffee.

How would you feel? Impressed like a special guest with a special connection and a sense of familiarity? Or violated because a perfect stranger knows your habits?

It's a fine line between the personal touch and the overly familiar, and where that line is varies enormously from person to person. It is up to the retailer to figure out if and how recognizing a regular customer in other retail outlets improves customer connections.

Getting Started

Retailers can start with basic blocking and tackling, a big data capable device in the hands of the sales team that puts fast visual answers about the customer in front of them. There also needs to be a new sales engagement process that uses facts to enhance the customer experience.

Consider setting goals to capture real, observed facts recorded in basic human terms that are easy to understand. Set rules on how to engage customers without offending them.

So what do you need to deliver results?

If we as customers see the benefit of leveraging big data and actionable intelligence to make on-the-spot decisions and amplify our own experiences, then why don't we as business leaders do it, too?

The Starbucks Experience

In the United States, Starbucks has created a customer loyalty card management app that:

- Links your Starbucks cards to your phone and allows the phone to be used to make purchases
- Allows customers to see what amenities a particular Starbucks store has before entering
- Remembers your favorite coffee, drink, and food items.

In exchange for this convenience, Starbucks gets to know:

- The user's past transactions, including regular purchases and stores visited
- The location of the user, if they opt into sharing this data

But why not develop this app further to collect more valuable data that would enable the firm to amplify the customer experience? When a customer carrying the app sits in a particular Starbucks outlet, the app can also collect information such as:

- How long the customer sits in the store and activities they do
- What searches and websites they visited
- What are their favorite music genres bases on their downloads

Right now the first movers can seize opportunities that their competitors don't even know about at a very low cost. Even collecting and leveraging the basic actionable intelligence delivers results far ahead of the competition. First movers are able to connect with customers and make them feel so comfortable that they want to come back and thus increase loyalty and awareness. This translates to higher margins and volumes. As the early mover, you are ahead. You can be the one with the competitive advantage.

However, the same is not promised to those who wait for the cost to come down. The benefits decrease as the playing field levels, and actionable intelligence becomes a must-have to survive as opposed to a way to win.

Summary and Considerations

Point to Ponder: The data industries are collecting can be used to deliver uniquely positive customer experiences.

Quote to Remember: "Intelligence can no longer just be restricted to specialists; it has to be accessible for everyone."

Questions to Consider: Are you going to start now to gain big benefits? Or wait and face the risk of elimination?

Notes

1. TED Talk transcripts, retrieved October 2013, www.ted.com/talks/shyam_sankar_the_rise_of_human_computer_cooperation/transcript.
2. Monte Williams, November 4, 1999, www.nytimes.com/1999/11/04/nyregion/danny-glover-says-cabbies-discriminated-against-him.html.

Chapter 11

Epilogue

At the beginning of this book, I told you the story of my mother, and how the experiences we had at two different hospitals when she fell critically ill demonstrated—in no uncertain terms—the power of actionable intelligence. My hope is that once you get to this part of the book you have the same kind of appreciation and, importantly, some pragmatic recommendations and tools that will help you very quickly and effectively implement an actionable intelligence strategy at your own organization.

I wish I could end the book by telling you that after my mother was cared for by the good doctors at Columbia she pulled through and went on to experience good health for years. We were able to take her from Columbia and place her in a wonderful long-term care facility in Queens, New York. And we did get some more time with her, praying, singing, and even watching episodes of her favorite show, *Murder, She Wrote*. She couldn't participate, but she was there, and when she smiled it brightened the entire world for me.

My mother passed in December 2010. She was a believer in Christ, a prayer warrior for our family, and a lovely person. We sent her off to heaven with a celebration at Memorial Presbyterian Church in New York. Alan Singer, her colleague and professor at Hofstra University, wrote a wonderful obituary about her on the *Huffington Post*. Hundreds of people came to her funeral, and many shared how she had touched their lives.

One of the dreams my mother had was to write a book. She had written and published books in the 1970s, and wrote curriculum in the 1990s. We talked about the book in passing conversation for about five years, but we never had time to discuss it in a focused manner. We were just both too busy. In a cruel twist, she had all the time in the world to write after she had her stroke, but had lost the ability to do so.

I miss my mother, and she continues to be an inspiration to everything I do and lives on in my children and me.

One of her final gifts to me was perspective. From her experience I learned the need to follow your dreams—right now, today. When the National University of Singapore invited me to lecture, I jumped at the opportunity and moved with my family to Asia. I had always wanted to live in that part of the world, and, after 13 years in New York, it was a good time for my wife to return to her family, who live there. I also looked forward to the rigorous education that I knew my children would get in Singapore's public schools.

I consider all of the good things that are happening to me in my life products of actionable intelligence. I also know that my ability to effectively deal with any bad things is a direct result of actionable intelligence. So, you can see why I am such an ardent evangelist.

I hope that you can follow your own dreams, and that one of them is to deliver—and live by—actionable intelligence!

Four Steps of Actionable Intelligence

I know how valuable your time is, and I truly hope that the moments you spend with this book provide a significant return on investment—both now and in the future as you apply the model across business functions, processes, and roles, and as you share the model with colleagues and partners up, down, and across the chain.

If there is one thing that you take away and share with colleagues in all areas of your business ecosystem, it is the SWAT framework. Taking the time to work through those four simple yet highly effective steps will help your business cut through the big data complexity and hype to get to the heart of the matter: relevant, contextual, meaningful information that you can use to make strategic decisions.

S	Ask strategic business questions	• What is the "burning platform" at my company?
W	Wrangle data	• What is the strategic business question? • Where can the data be found? • What are the IT infrastructure tools and policies needed? • Who in the company has the required skill set to analyze the data? • How can this data wrangling be done in a cost-effective way?
A	Answer with visualization	• What tools will help me best visualize the data? • How will the answer be used? • What report types/content are needed across business disciplines? • How will standard operating procedures change? • Are the right critical issues being highlighted for review?
T	Take action	• What actions can we take right now? Can we capture the value saved or earned? • Does the current process and organization need to change to start making fact-based decisions?

Remember that the first answers generated by the SWAT framework will help you and your colleagues develop more and deeper questions. The trick is to quickly start the SWAT process again to come up with answers to those questions in order to equip your colleagues and business partners with a complete big picture.

About the Author

Keith B. Carter lectures, writes, invents, and mentors from industry and corporate experience. He teaches both executive education and undergraduate purchasing and materials management. He also delivers results by leading several industry/academic big data and sales and operations planning projects in retail, high-tech, transportation, and chemicals.

He is Visiting Senior Fellow of Decision Sciences at the NUS Business School, as well as principal advisor to KPMG and board member of Mentorica Technology Pte. Ltd. (a retail sales, mobile, big data solution provider) and board member of 1st Call Consulting, a competitive intelligence firm specializing in finance and supply chain. He recently received a patent on a financial intelligence tool design.

From 1999 to 2012, Keith worked for the Estée Lauder Companies' Global Supply Chain Center of Excellence, to improve the overall performance of the company. Keith has led global supply chain initiatives: supply chain intelligence, knowledge management, transformation governance, supplier collaboration, audit, and data management—all to achieve end-to-end supply chain visibility.

From 1995 to 1998 Keith Carter worked as a consultant for Andersen Consulting in New York, now known as Accenture. His clients included Goldman Sachs, Smith Barney, Solomon Brothers, and the state of New York.

Keith holds a master's degree in Business Administration from Cornell University and a bachelor's degree in Electrical and Computer Systems Engineering from Rensselaer Polytechnic.

He enjoys an exciting life with his wife and two boys, as a private pilot, fencer (sword fighting), and snowboarder.

More information can be found on LinkedIn or his website, www .keithbcarter.com.

About the Contributors

Donald Farmer is the QlikView product advocate, working with customers and partners to establish QlikView as the leading solution for business discovery. Donald has over 20 years of experience in analytics and data management. In that time, he has worked as a consultant, in start-ups, and as a leader of Microsoft's BI product teams. He is a speaker at many international events on business intelligence, data integration, and data management; a blogger; and an author of several books. In addition to his career in business intelligence, Donald has worked in fields as diverse as fish farming and archaeology in Scotland. He is also a guest professor at South Western University in Chongqing, China, and advises on several academic boards. He lives near Seattle in an experimental woodland house, with his wife Alison, an artist.

He can be found on LinkedIn, Twitter (@donalddotfarmer), and his blog, www.donalddotfarmer.com.

Clifford Siegel is senior vice president of Lifetime Brands, a publicly traded company (NASDAQ: LCUT). He is an innovator who has

consistently delivered improvements to the company. He has successfully led:

- Integrations of acquisitions
- Improvements to supply chain business units
- Implementation of enterprise resource planning
- Delivery of actionable intelligence

Currently, he is completing ground-breaking capabilities in visualizing the compliance of suppliers to specifications, regulations, and supply
agreements.

He graduated from Northeastern University and Emerson College.
He has a wife and two children and lives in Long Island, New York.

QlikView provides a powerful, accessible business intelligence solution
that enables organizations to make better and faster decisions. QlikView
delivers enterprise-class intelligence and search functionality with the simplicity and ease of use of office productivity software. The in-memory associa-
tive search technology it pioneered makes calculations in real time, enabling
business professionals to gain insight through intuitive data exploration.
Unlike traditional business intelligence products, QlikView can deliver
value in days or weeks rather than months, years, or not at all. It can be
deployed on premise, in the cloud, or on a laptop or mobile device—from a
single user to large global enterprises. QlikTech is headquartered in Radnor,
Pennsylvania, with offices around the world (www.qlik.com).

Lifetime Brands is North America's leading resource for nationally
branded kitchenware, tableware, home décor, and lifestyle products.
Its products make it easier for you to prepare food, serve meals, entertain
guests, and decorate your home. It offers brands you trust, value without
compromise, and an unwavering commitment to innovation.

The company markets its products under such well-known kitchenware
brands as Farberware®, KitchenAid®, CasaModa®, Cuisine de France®,
Fred®, Guy Fieri®, Hoffritz®, Kizmos™, Misto®, Mossy Oak®, Pedrini®,
Roshco®, Sabatier®, Savora™ and Vasconia®; respected tableware brands
such as Mikasa®, Pfaltzgraff®, Creative Tops®, Gorham®, International
Silver®, Kirk Stieff®, Sasaki®, Towle Silversmiths®, Tuttle®, Wallace®, V&A®,
and Royal Botanic Gardens Kew®; and home solutions brands, including
Elements®, Melannco®, Kamenstein®, and Design for Living™. The
company also provides exclusive private-label products to leading retailers
worldwide (www.lifetimebrands.com).

Index